LIFE PLANS ON DIVE BAR NAPKINS

Published in 2021 by Hardie Grant Books an imprint of Hardie Grant Publishing

Hardie Grant Books (Melbourne)
Ground Floor, Building 1, 658 Church Street
Richmond VIC 3121, Australia

Hardie Grant Books (London)
5th and 6th Floors,52–54 Southwark Street
London SE1 1UN, United Kingdom

www.hardiegrant.com.au

Hardie Grant acknowledges the Traditional Owners of the country on which we work, the Wurundjeri people of the Kulin nation and the Gadigal people of the Eora nation, and recognises their continuing connection to the land, waters and culture. We pay our respects to their Elders past, present and emerging.

A catalogue record for this book is available from the National Library of Australia

Life Plans on Dive Bar Napkins / author, Paul Manser
ISBN: 9781743797464
Manser, Paul.
Travel journalists – Australia – Biography

Publication commissioned and managed by Courtney Nicholls
Edited by Carolyn Leslie, AE
Designed by Dallas Budde and Vaughan Mossop
Original design by SuSu Studio
Printed in China by Leo Paper Group

Author's note: To preserve people's identities, some names have been changed, some details may be hazy, or remembered by others a bit differently...

LIFE PLANS ON DIVE BAR NAPKINS

PAUL MANSER

Hardie Grant
BOOKS

This book is for Bruno. The grumpy little sausage dog I left behind, the one I always wished could come along too.

To all my friends who I have travelled with, or who have given me a couch to sleep on and cold beer after a long-haul flight, thank you. You have shared some of the best times of my life and had to deal with me hungover more than once.

Special thanks to my partner, Jane, and my parents for being so supportive and patient.

Thanks as well go out to Mike, Lesley, Dane, Kasia, Courtney, Dallas and Marion for all your help hacking through the verbose mess of my initial drafts and making the final collection of stories look so good. There would be no book without you.

Paul Manser is a Melbourne-based writer, traveller and drinker. Not necessarily in that order...

His works have been published in newspapers including *The Australian, Herald Sun, Courier Mail, MX* and *Sunday Telegraph* along with international media titles and travel brands including *MTV, Hearth Magazine, International Traveller* and *G Adventures.*

Paul can be reached at:

@paul_manser

DON'T LET THIS BOOK CONFUSE YOU... I'M NOT AN ADVENTUROUS PERSON.

I'm less '*Man vs. Wild*' and more 'man battling to find a hair product that survives the rigours of a sweaty nightclub at 3am.' I'm at the pointy end of evolution. Yet, if I didn't have a smartphone or credit card, I would be as useful in surviving day to day as a Valium-dependant sloth competing in an ultramarathon.

My hands have never experienced a callous. I cannot change a car tyre. I don't even have a car.

One time, I was riding a zip-line through the treetops on a mountain in New Zealand and everything stopped. Time. My heartbeat. All thoughts of what life will be like from that point on. Finished.

I struggled to not squeal. I even heard a eulogy being read faintly in the distance...

'GENIUS.'

'SO GOOD-LOOKING HE MADE ME CRY.'

'THE EMBODIMENT OF A MODERN RENAISSANCE MAN.'

But enough about the tributes unlikely to be uttered after my gloriously clumsy death. What you hold in your hands is a collection of experiences I wanted to get into print (but worried that some tut-tutting travel editor would strip of the best dick jokes). It's my travel tales the way I want to tell them.

You could say that this book is an unnecessary act of self-indulgence by an egotist who shirks life's responsibilities, drinks too much and thinks too little. And you'd probably be right.

This book is for those who travel to experience something different, who drink because they enjoy it, and whose life plans begin as incoherent scrawls on the back of a dive bar napkin.

Paul Manser
Melbourne, January 2022

2005 — 2021

THE HEADLICE OF HUMANITY

01

PALM SPRINGS, USA

Gareth and I are barrelling down the highway in a base-model grey Honda sedan when he lurches into a right-hand turn from the left-hand lane.

'Fuck me, that wind is hostile! Like a hungover café worker on a Sunday morning,' he says.

A red Mercedes convertible wears its black leather roof like an unnecessary fashion statement. The Mercedes's horn protests off-key, crying out like a reluctant bondage participant who forgot their safe word. Gareth chuckles and calls the driver an unremarkable, tone-deaf, anal wart.

A squall stirs the wispy sand. Random gatherings of fine powder look like poorly constructed sandcastles on the cooling early-evening bitumen. Roadside rock formations throw weak shadows in the dying light.

The grey Honda rocks as a crosswind insists itself on the driver's side of the vehicle. The wind rushes the desert plateau, spraying a gravel mist onto the windscreen and forcing our car to sway off the road.

Google Maps fades in and out of reception, losing our place in the world. A bluegrass country band sings about falling in love with a farm animal over the car stereo.

THE HORIZON IS VAST.

EMPTY

A roadside gas station advertises a free bottle of imitation cola with every full tank.

Gareth says, 'The driver of that Mercedes looked like a dentist. The headlice of humanity.'

'He probably possesses the personality of a plate of boiled algae,' I say. 'What if, hypothetically speaking, the Mercedes driver was an animal surgeon who helped crippled dogs walk again?'

'Well…' replies Gareth, 'that would make him a difficult man to hate, but it doesn't mean we shouldn't try.'

Wind turbines rise from the desert floor outside of Palm Springs. Their blades turn slowly, ignorant to the aggressive wind. A desert hawk swoops in and out of view, riding thermal currents through the sky.

We drive slowly down the main strip, past Hawaiian tiki bars and cabaret shows led by Barbra Streisand lookalikes. Middle-aged men (who could be Hollywood insiders) fall out of alcohol-stained supper clubs propped up by much younger women.

Even though the streets are full, Gareth says that it doesn't look like much is going on.

Downtown Palm Springs fights hard to overcome the stigma that its nightlife is centred around wealthy, middle-aged white women trying to reclaim their youth. The ladies can be found vomiting in the bushes after four martinis. Back in their hotel rooms, the husbands retire early to bed, getting ready for the early morning tee off on the golf course.

I'm still hungover from the night before. There are bruises on my legs and a raw, weeping wound on my knee. Last night, I had fallen off a boulder in Joshua Tree National Park. I had climbed the smooth, giant sculptured rocks on a dare from an army wife we had met at a roadside diner after drinking our liver's full of whiskey and beer.

I tell Gareth that I'm tired and want to go to bed. 'I neeeeeeeed sleep,' I moan as we pull into the driveway of our Airbnb.

The next morning, the world is a harsh, desolate place. Light sears my exposed eyeballs as I fumble around trying to extract my sunglasses from their protective case. Walking the streets, through the brightly paved canyons between expensively refurbished mid-century houses, it's as if every drop of moisture is being extracted from my skin.

I get back to the Airbnb and Gareth bursts out of the front door. 'Let's go and see some stuff before my morning coffee hits and I shit myself!' he yells.

Palm Springs is a memory of America at the height of its cultural influence. Its modernist houses hide their shimmering aqua swimming pools and architectural nuances discreetly behind high fences. The modular mid-century structures, open floor plans and panoramic views ooze an effortless decadence and outright confidence from a time when America wasn't a dysfunctional basket case.

The town whispers of an extravagant, hedonistic past.

The internet tells me that Palm Springs was the out-of-town hideaway favoured by the stars of yesterday. Frank Sinatra, Elizabeth Taylor and Elvis Presley set up camp here, trying to get away from it all.

We pull up outside Marilyn Monroe's former house. A group of tourists stand on the edge of a flowerbed in the front garden taking photos, before the current homeowner tells them to move on.

We drive on towards the edge of town. Gareth takes a work call on loudspeaker.

'What?! They wanted a door at the back of the house and not a window? They can just climb out the window if they want to play outside that badly!' he shouts. Gareth groans and says he needs a drink. We turn the car towards the Ace Hotel & Swim Club.

DRINKING ISN'T JUST A PASTIME IN PALM SPRINGS, IT'S A FULL-TIME OCCUPATION.

The scene around the pool at the Ace Hotel & Swim Club resembles a glamorous hipster orgy. A young, beautiful crowd lounges about like extras in a fashion photo shoot. The men run their fingers over pencil-thin porn-star moustaches, talk about their favourite Brooklyn tattoo parlours and raise a pair of coloured Ray-Bans in the air when signalling the waitstaff for a drink.

The women all look like aspiring Victoria's Secret models. They splash in the shallows of the vast concrete pool. They pout with silicone-heavy lips and squeal when a phone gets dropped in the pool.

A DJ plays an eclectic mix of early Phil Collins and underground Japanese electro. When someone comes up to his booth to request a song, he says he doesn't have it.

Gareth orders a couple of mojitos in plastic cups from someone who looks like the drummer for The Strokes. The roaming bartender doesn't even look at us when taking our drinks order or our money, choosing instead to stare blankly at the mountains in the distance.

Gareth asks The Strokes Drummer if he got our order. 'Heard it all…' is the dismissive response.

I sink slowly into the crystal-clear, turquoise water, sunglasses perched on top of my head. The sweat from my body pollutes the pool like a small oil slick. I watch the petrol-hued droplets glisten on the surface as a man with a thick, sandy beard and slick-backed hair floats by. He instructs his girlfriend where to stand to get the best picture.

The Strokes Drummer returns with two Jack Daniel's and Coke. Clearly, he didn't hear our order, or care. Gareth takes the change and doesn't leave a tip. The DJ mixes 'The Boys of Summer' into an early Talking Heads track.

I STAND IN THE MIDDLE OF THE POOL, SLIDE ON A PAIR OF REFLECTIVE SUNGLASSES

AND BEGIN TO PISS...

HOW TO COOK A HUMAN

02 MALMÖ, SWEDEN

The message board post reads:

YOU:
Sweat rolled between your breasts. Your hairy nipples glistened under the muted fluorescent light, drawing attention like two sexually charged emergency beacons in a sea of bad men.

ME:
Mesmerised. Unable to talk, as someone poured water over hot coals. The room turned to steam, the door opened, and you were gone. Come back, my furry sauna stranger. Let's leave the hot tap running in my bathroom and watch each other stew.

I shouldn't be surprised. The only person to blame here is me. I was the one who clicked on craigslist's 'Missed Connections' while searching online for the best place to sweat out a weekend of bad choices in southern Sweden. Now I'm second-guessing a sauna visit, unsure how to react if I stumble into a steamy stand-off.

All I know is that I can't stay in this room. My hotel is the worst.

The carpet is eroding and stained. Fingerprints smudge a glass tabletop like a talentless child's finger painting.

The Wi-Fi connection drops out. Again. I would walk downstairs to complain if I wasn't so worried about the skinny, expressionless receptionist. He seems like the kind of guy who visits a morgue after-hours to peel apart chilled corpses and sew the skin together into human pyjamas, which he later sells online with the tagline: 'The Epidermis You Want to Be In.'

I walk into the bathroom where a permanent, unplaceable smell percolates in the shower basin. The skin on my face is grey and loose. Dark pits swallow my eyes. I grab a crumpled shirt off the tiled floor and take the stairs to the street below.

The early March sun touches the Malmö waterfront lightly. The sky is clear, but the solar rays are weak and ineffectual, like a rationally thought-out perspective in an argument on the internet. I walk along a wooden pier and enter the historic waterfront bathhouse and sauna, Ribersborgs Kallbadhus.

A small white towel is all that covers my manhood as I exit the bathhouse change room. This is my second attempt at visiting a sauna. The last time, I tried to enter the sauna wearing a modest pair of swimming shorts but was ushered out by an old man whose bare testicles bounced around his knees.

I push against the heavy wooden door. Stepping inside the sauna the heat is overwhelming. Another old man with droopy testicles is here. This one gives me a polite nod from across the room.

I take a seat on a lower step, heeding the bathhouse receptionist's advice that the higher you sit, the hotter you feel.

A middle-aged man with an 80s-inspired flat-top haircut scoops up a ladle of water and pours it over the hot coals. The rocks hiss in violent protest and throw out a boiling mist. He repeats the action twice more until it becomes hard to breathe.

I lean back against a wooden stair, faking a look of comfort. I am being boiled alive, my flesh firming and already medium-rare.

Yet, when I survey the room, everyone else seems unfazed by the extreme heat or rampant nakedness.

A rush of cool air. The sauna door opens. I worry a woman will enter and I'll have to spend the rest of my session sucking in my bloated belly.

A short, tanned man steps into the room and immediately takes a seat on the top stair. This impressive act of dominance unravels five minutes later when he suddenly exits the sauna, distressed and panting like a parched toy poodle on a summer's day.

A German complains that in his country, saunas are not segregated. Here, his wife is only allowed to bake herself in another room.

I let out a sigh and the circumference of my gut increases instantly. Sweat covers my skin like a greasy, toxic film. My body purges itself, smelling like bad vodka and regret. I wipe my arms down with the napkin-sized towel. The flat-top ladler pours water on the hot coals.

The German encourages him to be a man. The room temperature is 90°C and rising. Outside it is less than 10°.

I turn my head and it takes a minute for everything to come back into focus. Maybe I'm dying. Or at least partially cooked. I stumble towards the exit. As I open the thick, wooden door, the chilled outside air slaps me in the face. I need more.

I shuffle along a wooden deck – unsteady, unsure. Wobbling down the wooden stairs, I come to the sea's edge. Water laps at my ankles, so cold that it is like being attacked by a million tiny, electrified needles. I belly flop into the ocean and wait for the onset of cardiac arrest.

I float, pushing myself away from the staircase. Adrenaline surges through my body and it feels like I'm living two moments for the rest of the world's one. I drift alongside the giant timber pier, my heavy arms raising and falling without rhythm through the dark waters of the Öresund Strait.

KEEPING IT IN THE FAMILY

03

REYKJAVIK, ICELAND

'You bury me alive,' says a bored-looking girl sitting beside me at the bar, before yawning and turning away to start a conversation with her mobile phone.

The bartender picks up an empty glass and insists we've already met. I can't remember him. Tall, blond and no tan, looking like everyone else in this bar. And this city.

Tall, Blond and No Tan tells me, 'I also work as a concierge. I think I checked you into your hotel this morning. You asked if the sky was always grey.'

'Sorry. Thanks for the view of the carpark,' I say. I'm trying to sound humorous, but I'm coming across like a confrontational jerk. It's not surprising I can't remember him. I was barely awake when I arrived at the Hilton Reykjavik Nordica. The world was a loud, nauseating place that kept asking if I needed help with my bags, or a wake-up call.

Ice is left exposed at the bottom of my glass. Tall, Blond and No Tan swoops on the empty vessel like an outer-suburban fighting enthusiast on a Monster Energy drink two-for-one sale. He refills my drink before I've had time to decide if I want another.

The bar is occupied by people who look like they just walked out of a casting call for *High Cheekbone Monthly*.

Tall, Blond and No Tan asks why I'm in Iceland. 'I'm emotionally damaged and looking for love,' I blurt out, instantly regretting my answer. The bored girl beside me gets up and walks away.

Fun fact 1: With little over 300,000 people, Iceland is Europe's most sparsely populated nation, leaving plenty of room for uninterrupted views of screensaver-worthy waterfalls, polar ice flows and tragic *Game of Thrones* fans looking for love North of the Wall.

Fun fact 2: I was living in London and fresh out of what could loosely be termed a 'relationship' with an alcoholic primary school teacher. Scrolling through internet travel sites, I saw a special for an off-season, four-day holiday in Iceland for £399. In my drunken haze, I read this as £39.99. Slight difference.

I don't know why I came to Iceland. I mean, besides misreading an internet travel deal. Maybe it was because a friend told me that Icelandic people were so aesthetically pleasing that I may as well have my eyeballs surgically removed at the airport departures lounge, because anyone I saw after I departed Reykjavik would be a disappointment.

The warm sting of straight liquor fills my mouth. Tall, Blond and No Tan laughs and wishes me luck. 'If you hadn't noticed, Icelandic women are not easy to approach,' he warns. 'Although your foreign status could work to your advantage.'

Given its isolation and limited gene pool, dating in Iceland has its challenges. On top of the regular dating concerns, including the possibility your passionate night of romance could end with you in an ice bath (minus a kidney), Icelandic singles also must also stop and ask themselves...

'AM I ABOUT TO SLEEP WITH MY COUSIN?'

Tall, Blond and No Tan pulls out his phone. He wants to show me a new app that helps Icelandic people avoid sleeping with a direct blood relative. Handy.

'The Incest Prevention app uses a genealogical database of Icelandic peoples. Users can bump their phones together to find out if they are related,' Tall, Blond and No Tan explains.

'This is your angle', he urges. 'You are not on the app.'

He points out a cute brunette on a sofa in the far corner of the bar.

Cute Brunette's on her phone, probably consumed with worry that she will see her next lover at some family reunion. I walk over and cough to get her attention. She looks less than impressed at having a mist of saliva sprayed into the air above her.

At this point, I realise Cute Brunette is far too good-looking for me.

'You won't find me on there,' pitching my voice high. She doesn't respond.

I drop my voice low and say slowly, 'You won't find me on your app. There's no way we're related.'

Her eyebrows arch high. The deep, black pupils of her eyes widen.

Cute Brunette asks, 'Why would you assume I thought we were related?'

She turns her phone screen around. 'I'm looking up tropical flesh-eating diseases for a research project.'

'Well, you won't find me in there either,' I say. 'Can I buy you a drink?'

Cute Brunette stops. She places her phone down.

She considers the last two minutes carefully, before politely saying, 'No. And not because you might be my cousin. Or because I am worried that I may catch some skin-eroding condition from sitting near you. I just don't want to have a drink with you because you actually seem a bit weird.'

A DRUNK'S COURAGE

04

TOKYO, JAPAN

カラオケ館
2F
第一マツヤビル
96
キューログ
薬
5%値引き
SALE
ダイコク
学生限定
フリータイム
880
1480

Smoke fills the room. It coats my lungs with every breath I draw. The ghostly vapour from a roll-up cigarette billows out of the bartender's mouth like the smokestack of an industrial factory. Her voice is raspy and breaks halfway through sentences. She moves on instinct at the sound of ice rattling at the bottom of an empty glass.

Elbow real estate on top of the bar is at a premium. Rows of sake, international whiskies, local Japanese beers and takeaway tempura take up most of the surface area.

A bottle of local apricot liquor is pushed under my nose. I take a mouthful. And then another. The chain-smoking bartender's thin layer of make-up does little to conceal the fact she was serving until 6am this morning. Dark circles trace the outline of the Chain Smoker's tired eyes.

The bar is full. It is impossible to walk to the small bathroom without getting physically intimate with the other patrons. Conversations are shared between strangers and swigs of hard liquor. Before I order another drink, the bartender closes the door to the outside world. There is no space for newcomers. It's a full house.

There are six people inside the bar.

Tucked away in a small area of the Shinjuku district is a collection of ramshackle buildings that house more than 200 tiny bars along six narrow alleyways. Full of local musicians, filmmakers, artists and first-class alcoholics, Golden Gai is a glimpse into Tokyo's past. It is a celebration of a city and its people from a time before the country's 'economic miracle.'

Getting a drink in Golden Gai is not easy. Many of the bars do not welcome tourists and some only ever serve regular customers. Blind luck and ignorance got me in the front door of this one. I sat down before anyone could protest about my presence and by then everyone was too polite to ask me to leave.

I share bar space with a local architect. Every ten minutes, the Chain Smoker taps a sculptured fingernail on the side of The Architect's glass. The thin plastic echo reminds The Architect that his drink is getting warm and the Chain Smoker's wallet is not getting any fatter.

The Architect has a soft American accent from his years studying in California. 'Do you know why Golden Gai is so special?' he asks.

'Tokyo has been reborn many times over the last century. From an earthquake in 1920s, to bombing raids of World War II. Our city's architectural heritage has been ruined. But Golden Gai is different. Somehow it survived...'

'New Tokyo was built by the colourblind; soulless grey concrete towers dominating the city's skyline. Along with losing our architectural memory, something of Tokyo also got lost along the way,' he laments.

'People are afraid to be themselves. They create fantasy lives and dress like ridiculous cartoon characters in order to fill something that is missing. Something that is real.'

I ASK THE ARCHITECT, 'WHAT IS

小松ビル
お好み焼
本陣
8F
すずや
DOUTOR
DOUTOR
DOUTOR
kawara CAFE & DINING
熟成和牛焼肉
Aging Beef
新橋
魚金
ちびすけバル
たばこ
酒
銀行ATM
OKONOMIYAKI
お好み焼き本
The Corner 117
4F
お好み
もんじゃ
たこ焼き
7F
小松ビル
3F
麻雀
ブル
6F
お好み焼
本陣
8F
お好み焼き本陣
2F
歌舞伎町一番街
Loco
劇場通り
ELEVEN

He rolls a cigarette and replies, 'This. This conversation. This place. This is real.'

The Architect tells me, 'Today Japan is so scared of itself that people live their lives online. We have restrictive security measures that limit daily life. I mean, shit – there aren't even rubbish bins on the streets because people are worried that they could be targets for terrorism.'

The Chain Smoker moves The Architect's drink away from him when he isn't looking.

'Have you heard the story of how Golden Gai nearly burned to the ground?' she asks.

The Chain Smoker cleans a whisky glass. During Japan's construction boom of the 1980s, it was common for the Japanese mafia, or Yakuza, to set fire to properties. They would burn down whole city blocks so they could sell the wasted land to scheming property developers. The Golden Gai and the land it sat on was a prime target.

'The Yakuza in Japan are very powerful,' the Chain Smoker whispers. 'They are everywhere. Control everything.'

The Architect chimes in, 'Don't underestimate a drunk's courage. They were the ones who stood up to the Yakuza when it looked like everything might be burned to the ground. The bar owners and regular drinkers guarded the area. With a metal pole in one hand and a half-full bottle of sake in the other, they overcame the mob.'

A university-aged girl, with a fringe so long she has to angle her face upwards just to look people in the eye, asks if I have plans for dinner. The Fringe says, 'I know a great place that makes soba noodles by hand.'

Moving her delicate wrists unconsciously in a folding pattern, The Fringe has a dreamy, faraway look in her eyes as though she is remembering something pleasant.

The Chain Smoker gives The Architect back his drink. It is impossible to leave this place in any hurry. Golden Gai feels like old Tokyo, somewhere time came and went without fuss and people and conversation mattered.

The Chain Smoker changes the record and Nina Simone starts to splutter from a speaker. I sip at a brown liquid that could remove bloodstains from a serial killer's car boot. The Chain Smoker asks, 'Anyone hungry if I order some food?' Waves of needy, hungry hands rise without hesitation.

She orders takeaway for everyone. Conversation fades and the noise of chopsticks doing battle over communal sashimi rises.

With our stomachs a mess of raw fish and alcohol, The Architect and I pay our bills and part ways.

Walking down a narrow alley out of Golden Gai, I see a group of men in spoiled suits fall out of a bar. They resemble the finishing line of a marathon: bleary-eyed, with colourless faces, stumbling and shifting on unsteady feet.

Judged against the hushed, nicotine-stained conversations of Golden Gai, the harried streets of central Tokyo are madness. Colossal towers of glass and concrete surround me. The harsh neon lights burn holes into my brain. There are people everywhere. The air is polluted with the noise of bad karaoke and a hundred computer games being played simultaneously.

I approach a group of women to ask if they know where my hotel is. Their English is broken, and my Japanese is terrible.

One of the women, dressed as a fairy princess, adjusts her wings and makes a series of hand gestures pointing the way.

I thank them and ask if they know where I can throw away my empty water bottle. Fairy Princess says, 'Take it with you. There are no rubbish bins on the street.'

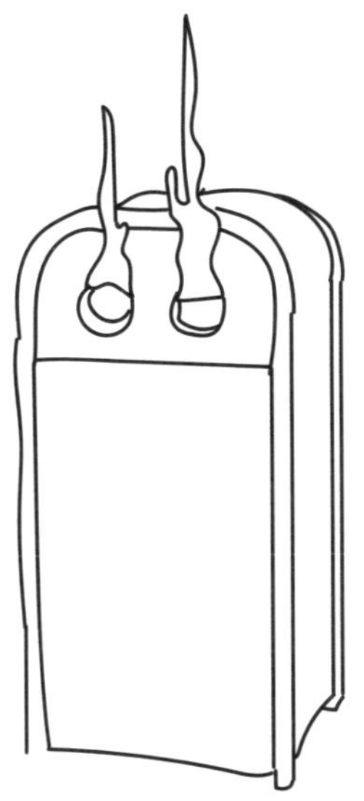

PEOPLE ARE AFRAID OF EXPLODING RUBBISH BINS IN THE NEW TOKYO.

HUNKY JESUS

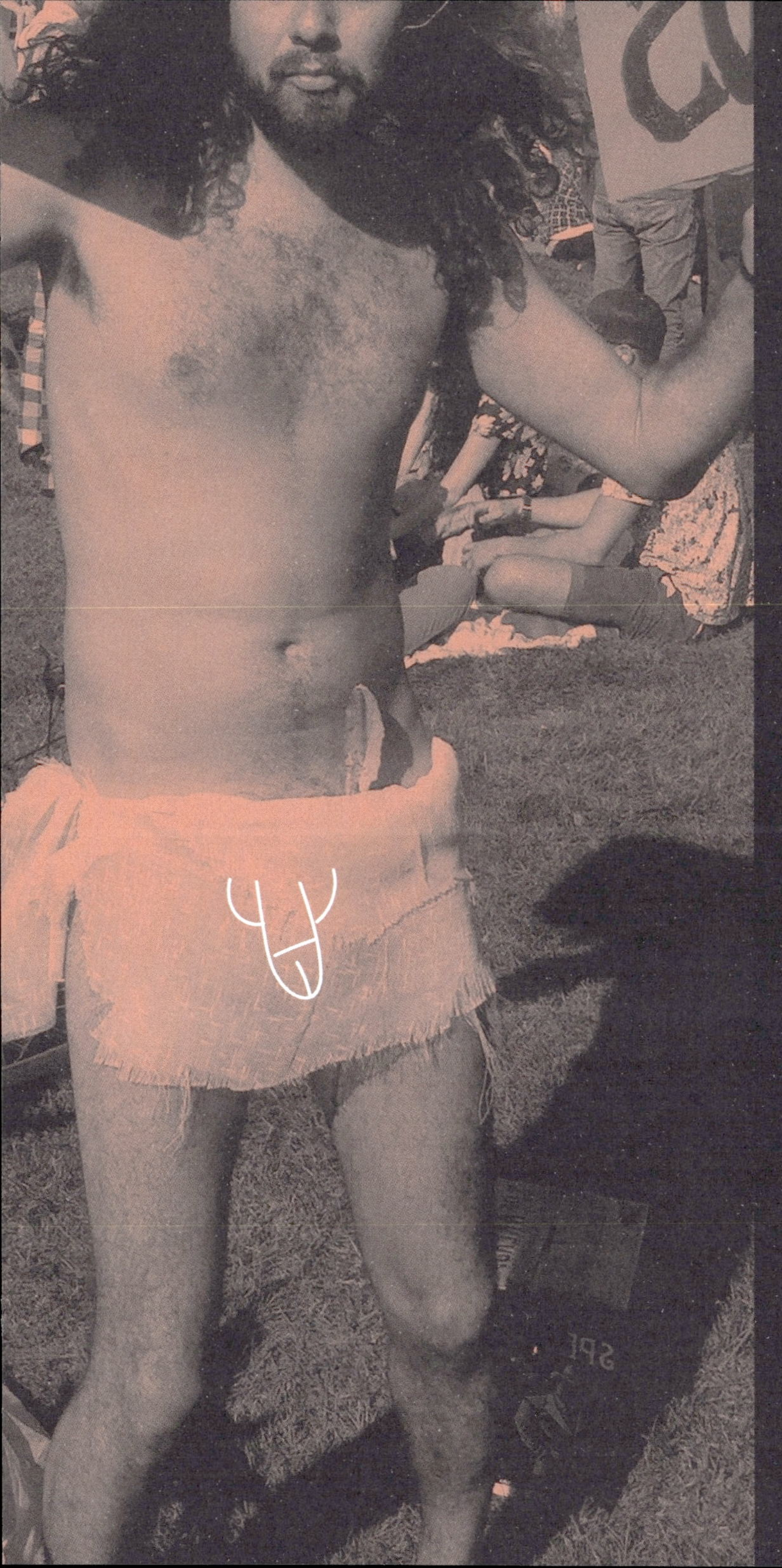

05

SAN FRANCISCO, USA

His body hangs from the wooden cross, barely moving. The side of his chest looks like it has been clawed by a feral cat. Flies flock to the thick, crimson pools of blood.

The air is heavy with violence. Thick iron nails appear to puncture his palms. A thorny crown cuts into the flesh around his skull.

The late afternoon sun sits fat on the horizon.

The skin on his face is etched with painful creases. His mouth appears twisted in a scream, but no sound comes out.

The end cannot be far away.

A crowd of wide-mouthed onlookers stare in morbid fascination as if driving slowly past a fresh car crash. The man on the cross slumps forward and his eyes roll back in his head. Everything moves in slow motion, like time itself railed a line of ketamine.

Suddenly his chest heaves and struggles through a tortuous breath.

A shout pierces the hushed voices. 'Take it off Hunky Jesus... Take it all off!' The crowd screams in approval.

A disco beat starts up in the distance. Hunky Jesus Contestant Number 5 steps down off his cross. He struts across the stage, gives a sudden turn and pouts to the waiting pack of smartphone cameras clamouring for clear airspace.

The social media paparazzi frantically shoot, filter and upload what is likely to be the unholiest post of the year. Someone yells '#SweetJesus' over the loudspeaker.

Beside me, an app designer in his mid twenties wearing a puffer vest and yellow-tinted sunglasses lights up a menthol cigarette.

Sister Titty Gang Bang, a statuesque drag queen painted white with a flowing mane of purple feathers, picks up a microphone and asks the crowd, 'Who here would sin for Jesus Number 5?'

The massed people cheer wildly.

To the uninitiated, San Francisco's annual Hunky Jesus competition can come across as a celebration of absurdity, parodying religious organisations with a history of refusing to accept the gay community. The competition has been held every Easter Sunday for more than 35 years, aiming to convert people from 'Our Lord and Saviour' to 'Our Lord and Sexy.'

'For the first-timers here today, don't worry, we'll be kind. And for the regulars whose sorry faces we see year after year... behave,' Sister Titty Gang Bang says. 'If you did not know, the Hunky Jesus event is a birthday party for the Sisters of Perpetual Indulgence. It's also a way for gay people who identify as Christian to celebrate a more accepting version of the holy saviour. One with a healthy sense of humour.'

Like much of San Francisco's progressive community activism, what used to attract the ire of large sections of the local religious society has grown to become a much-loved community fixture.

On the stage, a short, bearded man with thick gold earrings that could have been stolen from the grave of a 16th-century, wooden-legged pirate hushes the crowd.

Pirate MC says, 'You've marvelled at Twerk It Jesus and seen Redneck Jesus pollute the stage. It's now time to book a fierce perm, sew a pair of thick shoulder pads into your leather jacket and stand in front of a glitter cannon... because here comes Glam Rock Jesus!'

Glam Rock Jesus kicks the air like he's the lead singer in a Def Leopard tribute band. He jumps around the stage as if someone lined his underwear with cayenne pepper. Metal adorns his shoulder pads. The neckline on his gold dress plunges halfway down his chest.

The app designer stamps his cigarette out on the matted grass of Golden Gate Park. He tells his friend about a new brunch place in the Tenderloin district that does bottomless mimosas on a Sunday.

'It has a large patio that catches the mid-morning sun, but the crowd is very 'yachty', like everyone stepped out of a Ralph Lauren store,' App Designer moans.

The next contestant onstage is Bad Santa. He urges Glam Rock Jesus off the podium with a giant candy-striped cross. Bad Santa wears a pair of festive red underwear... and nothing else. He has a thick, tangled mess of white hair covering his back.

He boasts to the crowd, 'I've got the biggest sack going around!'

A new moon is rising in the sky like an overzealous friend arriving unfashionably early to a party. Up on stage, Pirate MC brings all the contestants back onto the stage. The winner is about to be determined by the noise of the crowd.

Glam Rock Jesus achieves a modest roar. I add my voice to those calling for Bad Santa to take home first prize, or at least a shirt to cover his back. But when Twerk It Jesus re-emerges to gyrate his hips across the stage again, the crowd erupts.

As Twerk It Jesus proceeds to bless his newfound followers with a continuous series of hypnotic pelvic thrusts, Pirate MC bellows 'We have our winner... '

'ALL BOW DOWN FOR THE SECOND CUMMING OF CHRIST'

SOME-WHERE BETTER TO BE

06 LOS ANGELES, USA

The sun sinks into a low-rise skyline. Concrete buildings resemble lonely monolithic sculptures bathed in a pale yellow light. A late afternoon gust announces itself on Sunset Boulevard, forcing palm trees to lean above crowded sidewalks.

Oscar takes a long look over a short wine list. The waitress with visible, store-bought hair extensions has somewhere better to be. She silently mouths lines for her next audition in-between scribbling down drink orders.

I assume that she tells her parents things are going great when they call to check in once a week from San Antonio, before asking if she can borrow money to make rent.

Like a mosquito drunk on summer's blood flying towards a fluorescent blue bug zapper, LA is a magnet for the insecure and the desperate-to-get-ahead. Jump in any Uber and before you know it, you are listening to the CV of a struggling actor who played a sexually confused lifeguard on *Baywatch* for two episodes in the 90s.

Oscar says that he is over online dating. 'I just can't deal with it anymore. Too many freaks and false advertisers,' he declares, sounding older than he should.

Hair Extensions stands over us scribbling notes. Oscar says, 'I swear to god. My sex life had better not be used in some third-rate acting-school skit next week.'

She walks away, and one glance at Oscar tells me that I will be the one left paying the whole tip.

I need to leave. Cooper has booked a table at Chateau Marmont. Or rather, Cooper's girlfriend – who works for a talent agency and says coming home drunk after midnight on a Tuesday is part of her job – booked us a table at Chateau Marmont.

I say goodbye to Oscar, leave a pile of bills and apologise to Hair Extensions on the way out.

I'm running late and getting around LA can be a hot mess. The city is impossible to cross in peak-hour traffic, so I walk the few blocks to meet Cooper.

Cooper waits for me on the roadside wearing a pressed white long-sleeve shirt, looking like someone who would get mistaken for a daytime TV actor in a domestic airport lounge. I'm wearing an ill-fitting blue and pink checked shirt...

I LOOK LIKE A FAT TABLE CLOTH.

Cooper says the Chateau Marmont oozes with old-world Hollywood glamour like a freshly burst rectal cyst. It's where A-grade celebrities go to behave like D-grade people. Led Zeppelin rode motorcycles through the lobby in the 1960s and it was the first venue to ban Lindsay Lohan in the early 2010s.

We queue up, waiting to have our names checked at the door.

The patio at the Chateau resembles a glorified catering tent at a financially responsible cousin's wedding. We take our seats under the white gazebo, order some drinks and settle in as Salma Hayek walks past, looking like an erotic penguin in a black jumpsuit.

'Did I tell you about the doco we're filming in Costa Rica next month?' Cooper asks, knowing that I'll become instantly jealous.

A man with the facial skin of a leather belt and hair like a peroxide lion's mane pulls up to our table with a friend. Swelling beneath a tight tan suit, he could have been a wrestler or solarium spokesman in a past life.

The Solarium Spokesman says, 'I'm a producer and this guy is the head of programming for a TV network you all would watch.' The Solarium Spokesman points at his friend, announcing their CVs without being asked. Head of Programming helps himself to our bottle of 2012 Napa Valley rosé without asking.

A girl at our table wears a denim jacket and has teased her hair in a way that makes her look like she walked off the set of a Cyndi Lauper music video. She stares at the gold and jewel-encrusted rings on the Solarium Spokesman's fingers.

The rings are excessive. They're the kind of thing Roman emperors would have worn while their stabbing political rivals. Solarium Spokesman removes the largest ring, featuring a huge emerald stone, and leans over to place it on her finger. It swims around her bony knuckle, dominating the landscape of her hand.

'How does it feel to wear part of Hollywood history?' he asks. 'That was the ring Liberace was wearing when he died.'

Cyndi Lauper Hair flashes a thin, fake smile and thanks the Solarium Spokesman. But it is clear she feels uncomfortable wearing the ring of a dead man. And that she has no fucking clue who Liberace was.

Head of Programming downs more of our rosé and looks around the patio for an escape. He makes eye contact with an elderly lady at another table.

'SO, YOU MUST GET RANDOM PEOPLE PITCHING YOU TERRIBLE TV SHOW IDEAS ALL THE TIME...'

I say to Head of Programming.

'Why? Do you have something I might be interested in?' he asks, without enthusiasm.

I signal to the waiter that we need another bottle and reply, 'Your next summer blockbuster will be a TV series called *Love Blisters*.' Head of Programming raises his eyebrows.

'Go on,' he says.

'The premise,' I say, 'is for a new age dating show where two strangers go out for dinner and drinks. They get to know each other but before the night is over one party has to reveal that they have a life-long STI. Then the other party will face a decision of if to continue seeing the person, or not.'

Silence oozes out of Head of Programming. A waiter materialises with an ice-bucket. Cyndi Lauper Hair is begging Solarium Spokesman to take Liberace's death-ring back.

Cooper cleans his sunglasses with the tablecloth. Head of Programming stands and waves to the elderly lady at the other table. And Salma Hayek floats on by talking to someone who looks just like Matthew McConaughey.

07

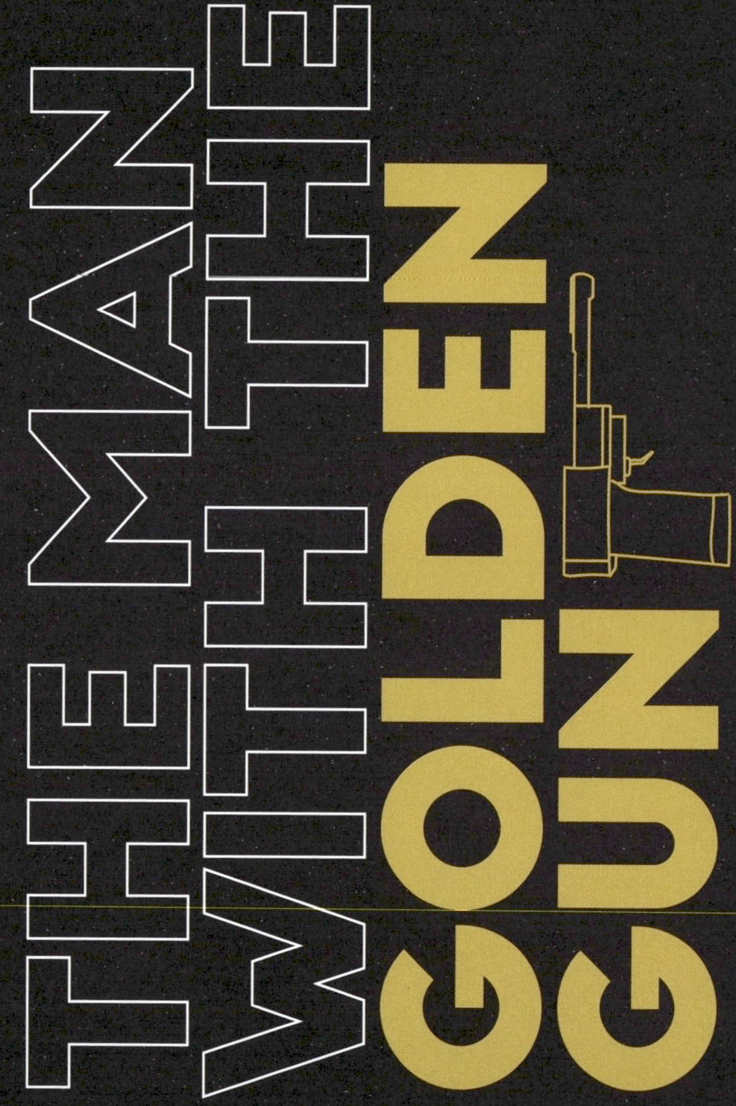

RIO DE JANEIRO, BRAZIL

Traffic slows. A police siren wails, piercing the silent standstill. There is blood on the highway. A cracked motorcycle helmet, newly splashed with crimson red, attracts flies from all around.

The distraught driver of the weathered fruit truck paces back and forth. He will never sleep the same again. The sun breaks through a thick bank of clouds and someone at the back of our bus mutters 'Welcome to Rio.'

The traffic solemnly marches past the flashing lights. Conversation is thin. A Sandra Bullock romantic comedy plays over the bus's entertainment system, but I gave up watching a long time ago. We take the exit ramp to Copacabana Beach.

All I want is a quiet night and some sleep, because tomorrow I will be visiting a favela.

Housing some of the poorest people in Brazil, the favelas are often mistakenly seen as a breeding ground of crime. And certainly not advisable for tourists to travel into alone.

I wake up the next morning, cursing the inventor of dark rum. My head is going to explode. The alarm on my mobile phone screams at me, telling me I only have 15 minutes until we leave. I throw on the t-shirt I was wearing the night before.

My memory shifts through images of a Bossa Nova club, tequila and dance lessons from a sixty-year-old local woman with wandering hands.

A van with tinted windows pulls up outside our hotel. I get in the back.

Our guide for the day has tattoos across her back. Tattoos on her legs. She lays out a few ground rules as we drive.

'The favela you are visiting today is called Rocinha. It is built on the side of a hill. Taking photos at the bottom of the favela is strictly prohibited,' she says.

'At the bottom of the favela, there are watchers who work for the local drug gang. They monitor everyone who comes into and leaves the favela. Police, tourists looking for drugs, rival gang members – they see it all.'

At the entrance to the favela, our van stops. We get out and blink against the glare of the mid-morning sun. A few locals glide past, eyeing our group.

Tattoos on Her Legs tells us, 'Get on the back of one of these motorcycle taxis. They know where to go. They will take us into the heart of the favela.'

I jump on the back of a red bike and put my arms around the portly taxi rider in front me. This elicits laughter from the riders around us. Taxi Rider pulls my arms down and motions to the small handles at the back of the bike. He mutters something in Portuguese that I can only assume translates to 'Not on the first date'.

Someone obviously has told Taxi Rider that they're giving away free doughnuts up the road because we're off like a rocket.

Crammed with cars, buses and motorcycles, the main road through Rocinha is a heaving mass of life and the main artery for trade among the locals. Taxi Rider swerves to miss potholes and brakes suddenly for a dog running across the road. He leans aggressively on the horn when a bus comes towards us on the wrong side of the road. There are electricity wires down across the road.

We come to an abrupt stop. Traffic backs up. A melody of horns and cursing flavours the air.

MY HEAD NO LONGER HURTS.

ADRENALINE IS A WONDERFUL THING.

Taxi Rider squeezes between a car and a bus and around the electricity wires. We arrive at our meeting point and I get off his motorbike.

We weave our way through a laneway lined with convenience stores, bakeries and shoe repairmen. The locals smile and wave like old friends. I want to like them but keep a strong grip on my digital camera. Like an insensitive dick who thinks everyone wants to rob him.

Tattoos on Her Legs stops. She motions for our group to climb a flight of stairs. We come out onto a large balcony. Beneath us sprawls a colourful carpet of concrete housing, spilling down the face of the hill onto to the freeway below.

'Look, I'll give you a little history,' Tattoos on Her Legs starts. 'Some of the older favelas in Rio de Janeiro were originally started by slaves over 150 years ago. They grew as unregulated housing areas for those without enough money to live anywhere else.

'Today many favelas are unsafe to outsiders. Police have little control. Drug gangs have ruined many peaceful areas. The gang that currently controls Rocinha is called Amigos dos Amigos (ADA) – or Friends of Friends. It has been run by a man in his mid-twenties since the previous leader was killed by police,' she continues.

'ADA is considered one of the less extreme drug gangs in Rio. They do not dismember people and leave their body parts on display in public to inspire fear, unlike some of their rivals.'

Walking through Rocinha, ADA's footprint is everywhere. On every major building, there is an ADA tag.

Tattoos on Her Legs says, 'For each area of the favela, there is a local strong man or 'manager' who works for ADA. He's charged with ensuring the smooth running of the area... If you have a problem, you go and see your area manager.'

I get the impression that the area manager is more enforcer than counsellor. And they subscribe to the 'Speak softly and carry a large semi-automatic machine gun' school of management.

We stop to eat in a local bakery. The woman working the ancient cash register smiles and laughs when I try to order. I end up with a passionfruit cake. I want to ask her if she feels safe living in the favela. I want to know how she feels about the drug gangs controlling her streets, but I already feel guilty. Like I am participating in some perverse form of poverty tourism. I swallow my words along with the cake.

A childcare centre sits towards the bottom of the favela. It has been set up by the proceeds of tours like ours. Tattoos on Her Legs says, 'As you come in, just be quiet. All of the children are under the age of five and some may be having a sleep.'

We enter the centre up an uneven set of stairs. The main corridor is painted mustard yellow and laughter comes from one of the rooms. The children look curious and cheeky. Their wide eyes take us in. Too young to walk, they are all outstretched hands and looking for mischief.

Outside I pass a group of young boys playing on plastic drums. They keep a steady rhythm and pass a bucket around for money. We empty our pockets and continue on our way.

Tattoos on Her Legs says hello to a local area manager. He gives us the thumbs up. He winks at one of the girls in our group.

It is remarkable how normal everything seems. Life moves on in the favela. No one runs scared through the streets. People go to work. They sleep. They fall in love.

They live.

Local Area Manager shares a joke with someone out of view.

My eyes pass over the scene. Normal. It all seems normal. Except, except...

Local Area Manager laughs. He smiles. All the while,

A GOLD PLATED MACHINE GUN SITS IDLE ON HIS LAP...

BUT NO ONE

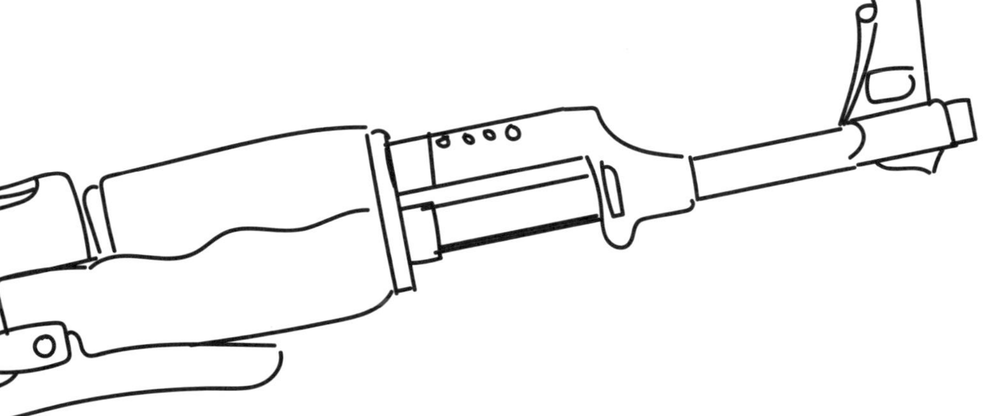

SAYS A THING.

MIKHA
GORBA
HAS A
CONCU

VANCOUVER, CANADA

IL

CHEV

Cloud ceiling. The city breaking a sweat. Lonely on a street corner, a man stands. The fading red embers of his cigarette float slowly in the air, like napalm snowflakes heading towards the worn grey concrete.

The man is pale, like wisps of smoke and winter. He rubs his hands with an alcohol-based sanitiser and serves slabs of processed meat on day-old buns to anyone with a few dollars in their pocket.

The taxi I travel in slows. The car's braking system sounds like the panicked wail of a cat having its tail pulled by a sadistic toddler who'll grow up to be successful lobbyist for the mining industry. Wafts of tepid hotdog water from the roadside vendor steal in through the taxi's half-opened windows, making me gag.

Airline tags hang from the suitcase on the seat beside me. They tell me I am in Vancouver, and I came via New Zealand.

Tim has left a key outside his apartment building for me. Upon arrival, a forensic search reveals that the keys are hidden under a pot plant brimming with stagnant, dirty water. It looks like the birthing place of a mosquito-borne, apocalyptic disease.

An angry wave of tiny insects fly into the air when I move the plant. I swallow at least three bugs and begin to worry that I'll die foaming at the mouth in under 20 minutes.

Tim arrives home from work at sunset. Shards of pale sunlight creep around the living room like a socially awkward religious conservative who's mistakenly stumbled into an orgy.

Through a window, a thin line of white clouds can be seen crowning the North Shore Mountains.

'You look like balls,' Tim says.

'I just swallowed three of your bugs and haven't slept in a long time,' I reply.

Tim wants to catch up over a beer. He asks, 'Have you been involved in black-market organ harvesting recently? If not, and you're still in possession of a liver, there are no excuses for not coming to happy hour.'

We take a short walk to The Narrow Lounge, a bar hidden off Main Street. With no signage, except for a flickering dull red light above the front door, the tucked-away bar looks as if it's been styled by a 1960s-style psychopath.

Dishevelled wallpaper, mounted animal antlers and a haunting chandelier give the impression you might go in for a drink and wake up tied in a basement, with Norman Bates smiling maniacally at you.

In daylight the bar's interior could be the height of distaste, but, with heavy lashes of alcohol and dim lighting, it's got just enough of a hidden thrift-shop vibe to draw in-the-know locals.

The volume of conversation rises through the bar as the night matures. I'm drinking dark rum like it's water and half listening to Tim as he offends anyone within earshot. His brash, questionable viewpoints on just about everything clearly mark him as a mad man.

'Vancouver's growing population of homeless people is the result of the city having warmer pavements to sleep on than Toronto,' he theorises between mouthfuls of tepid beer.

The bartender raises his eyebrows like his testicles have accidentally been placed in an ice bath. He shakes his head. We won't get served another round.

I tell Tim to lower his voice. He says, 'Chill man. Canadians are the friendliest people in the world. I haven't been punched in the face by one yet.'

I ask for our bill and carefully consider our topic of conversation when apologising to those around us. Tim stumbles to the bathroom.

I offer up my seat to a heavily bearded man wearing flannel who could either be a hardened lumberjack or an inner-city fine-arts student.

Emerging from the bathroom with a large purple mark spreading across his forehead, Tim yells, 'Stupid fucking toilet door. I headbutted it on the way out.'

'That bruise is massive. You look like Mikhail Gorbachev… on a bad day,' I say, before suggesting that we probably should get some food.

A cold wind blows down Howe Street. The moon fights to be seen from behind a crowd of silver clouds.

Two out-of-hours office workers loosen their ties and talk about pulling their bosses' eyelids off with rusted pliers as they eat slices of crispy white bread oozing with molten cheese.

I stand close enough to one of them to catch a nostril-full of aged cheddar before being handed a 'Jackson 3', which I am promised is the best grilled cheese sandwich in the world.

Mom's Grilled Cheese Truck is pretty much as the name advertises. Run by a larger-than-life lady called Cindy, it specialises in bread, cheese and grilling.

I burn the roof of my mouth with my first bite. By meal's end, there's a small pool of greasy cheese sitting in my lap like cooling lava.

We shuffle home past a forlorn hot dog seller leaning against his rusted metal truck. Tim puts a hand on my shoulder and begins talking gibberish. A piece of grilled cheese hangs from his mouth like a bungee cord for a thrill-seeking front tooth.

I look at Tim swaying and dribbling on himself and begin to suspect that he may be concussed.

Tim pokes the swelling dark purple bruise on the side of his head and swears loudly. He sighs and admits that maybe that knock on his head was harder than he first thought.

TIM IS UNSTEADY ON HIS FEET. HE SLURS, 'DOOOON'T WORRY. I'LL BE FINE. I'M FIIIIINE.

JUST DON'T LET ME FALL ASLEEP.'

UNPA
A DIS

09 LONDON, ENGLAND

CKING
ASTER

One way
N.W.A

A glass bottle explodes on impact, casting violent shards across bitumen. Slivers of shrapnel bounce off a grey Volkswagen Golf. A skinny teenager in a tattered Chelsea football jersey rides loose circles in the middle of the road. His mountain bike slips a gear when he stands to pedal, as he dares passing traffic to manoeuvre around him. The teenager sneers. He points at me and yells in a rapid-fire South London accent, 'Boy, I see you. I know where you live.'

Like a petrified meerkat spotting a hungry lion on the savanna, I scurry to the front door of our house. In the distance I can hear David Attenborough narrating the last minutes of my life. I wobble into the entrance juggling a hot chocolate, *The Times* and a bacon roll...

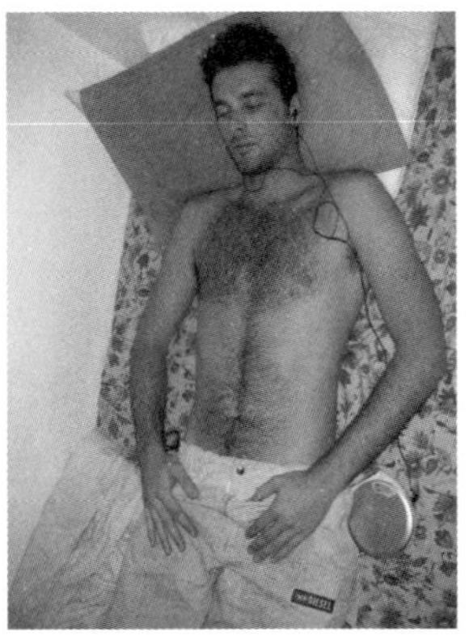

FUCKING LONDON.

There is a mattress in the hallway with an extremely large man asleep on it. He turns and snores, occupying an inconvenient amount of space. He's surrounded by four walls stained with damp. On the floor around him, recently spilled red wine colours the carpet.

It all looks a bit like a shit modern art installation, something that would attract the black turtleneck crowd.

EJ is on couch in an imitation Manchester United football jersey that he thinks no one can tell is fake. He's wrong.

EJ tells a story he heard from Sarah last night. 'Apparently, she used Alison's henna dyeing shampoo after a drinking a whole bottle of South African white wine. Sarah failed to see the difference between Alison's henna hair-dye shampoo and her own conditioner,' he says.

'Don't say anything when you see her. But her hair that used to be platinum blonde and is now mousy brown'.

Samuel Johnson said, 'When a man is tired of London, he is tired of life.' But, having lived in the city several centuries ago, Samuel Johnson didn't have to deal with hood rats looking to jump you for bacon rolls at 11am on a Sunday. He didn't consume the toxic fumes of summertime body odour on the Tube, or experience bartering body organs for a few pints of overpriced beer.

Don't get me wrong, London is amazing. It has drawcard tourist attractions like Big Ben, the Tate Modern, St Paul's Cathedral, Abbey Road Studios and that airline lounge where David Boon slept off the 52 beers he drank on a flight to the UK for the 1989 Ashes series.

But when you've done a few winters during which you start to question the existence of the sun, and the concept of a bed is a section of laminated floor in a two-bedroom apartment with 20 other tight-arsed Australians...

IT'S HARD NOT TO WONDER WHAT MIGHT BE NEXT.

Reid says that he desperately needs a favour. He didn't realise the time. He leaves London in a few hours and hasn't begun packing. Can we help?

EJ pushes rubbish from the floor to one side as he shuffles silently to the TV. I wipe my greasy, bacon-roll coated hands on the arm of the chair and try not to make eye contact.

Reid has lived in London for three years. He has accumulated a library of unnecessary junk and has had his flight home to Melbourne booked for months. And yet, only hours before take-off, does he begin to think about packing his life up.

Reid stands in front of the TV in a pair of fluoro-yellow jocks that he clearly stole from my room. EJ throws a cardboard coaster at Reid, but he won't move. There is a taxi coming to collect Reid in a half an hour and no way he can get everything packed.

The living room is a warzone.

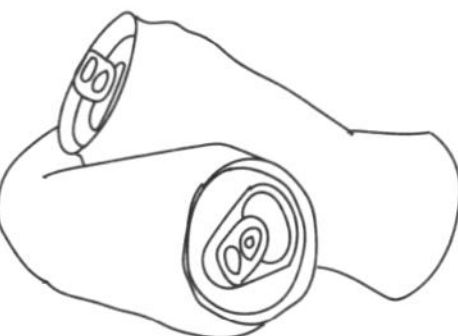

Half-empty cans of beer ooze their sticky insides out on the uneven wooden floor.

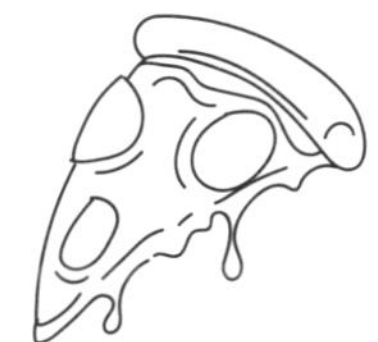

Half a pizza appears to be stuck to a wall.

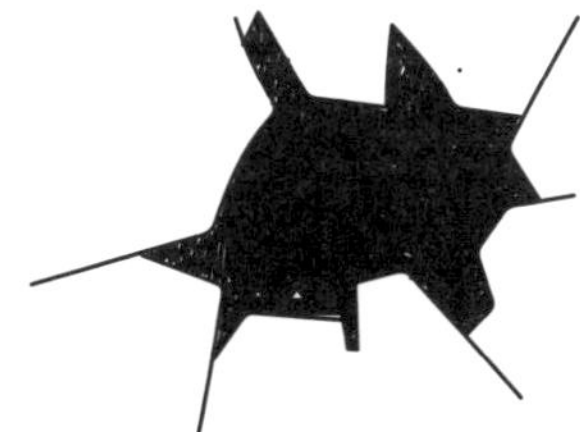

There's a fist-sized hole in the door.

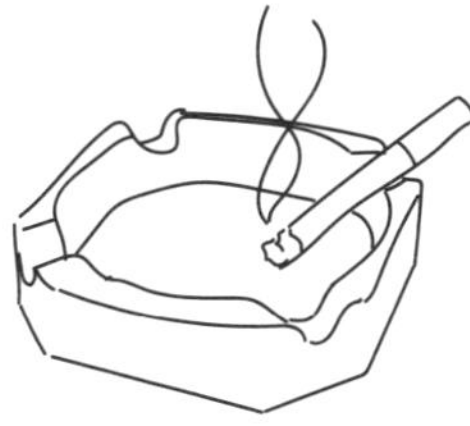

Cigarette ash coats every surface.

Reid begs us, 'Can't you get off your fat arses and help me out? Just go around the house and put anything that looks like it could be mine into this striped carry bag. Simple!'

Reid doesn't wait for a firm yes from EJ and myself before rushing out of the room to pack two other suitcases. EJ and I look at each other. The last thing we feel like doing is packing up Reid's life. We do need to do something about all the rubbish lying around the house though, and our council bins are already overloaded.

EJ gestures to Reid's cheap, striped plastic carry bag and smiles. He picks up a squashed beer can and throws it in the bottom of Reid's bag.

I tip in an ashtray full of cigarette butts.

Marvelling at our organisational genius, EJ and I begin to clean the house using Reid's luggage. The tops of pizza boxes, bottles of beer, hardened pasta – it all goes into Reid's carry bag. The living room floor emerges from its covering of rubbish.

A taxi horn squawks like a needy child outside the house. Reid's bag is three-quarters full. We find some clothing that may be his hanging from a doorway. We throw it on top.

Reid rushes up the stairs carrying two suitcases. He looks pale, stressed and like he hasn't had time to dry himself after a shower. The taxi driver takes Reid's bags and arranges them in the car around him.

EJ and I settle in for the afternoon on the couch. Manchester United are playing West Ham and when the camera pans over Wayne Rooney, EJ tries to compare him with Brad Pitt. 'Just look at the way he carries himself. He's the full package,' he says about the same freckled, balding, neck-less Wayne Rooney who better resembles the cartoon Shrek than a Hollywood star.

I drift in and out of sleep. Reid calls from the airport. EJ puts him on loudspeaker.

Reid yells, 'You're both fucking big hairy dicks! After I checked my bags in, airline staff called me back to ask if I had packed them myself. They were wondering why one of my bags was leaking beer on their conveyor belt and rattling like bottle shop'.

Reid sounds like he is about to have an aneurysm. 'I nearly didn't get let on the plane!' he screams.

He would not forget.

I laughed and realised that London wasn't so bad. I didn't need to go home. I didn't need to see Reid again, just yet.

WORLD
CUP

DON'T APPROACH A CELEBRITY WITH YOUR HAND IN YOUR UNDERWEAR

10

PAMPLONA, SPAIN

The road is cold and hard against my back. My face hurts. The side of my chest feels like it has been kicked by a football player. I hear voices in the distance, but my eyes refuse to open. Everything smells like a dirty toilet. My temples throb with a pain that only gallons of cheap, poorly manufactured red wine can inflict. The voices get closer. I feel a shoe nudge the soft flesh of my belly and hear the voice of a friend shriek in perverted delight. Kirsty asks in high-pitch excitement,

'PAUL, ARE YOU LYING IN PISS?'

I roll over and place an unsteady palm on the road. Shards of broken glass fall from my spoiled white t-shirt. A virgin morning sun bursts across the rooftops of Pamplona in northern Spain and the road is illuminated as a filthy, cobblestoned wasteland.

A roaming brass band erupts out of a side street. The trumpeters wave their instruments high in the air. The music is loud and off-key. A handful of drunken tourists dance behind the unexpected procession.

'Are you going to be ready?' Glen asks.

It is 7.30am and he wants to know if I'm going to run. I lean against a wall and everything starts spinning. I swallow a fresh mouthful of vomit.

'I can't run anywhere. Let alone outpace 30 tonnes' worth of bulls seeking to spear my insides,' I say. Today, he's on his own.

We stagger down pathways heavy with last night's rubbish. My feet push past empty beer bottles and plastic tubs of half-eaten paella.

A crowd of people surge against thick, wooden pylons, desperate for the best vantage point.

There are police everywhere, thumbing their black batons and eyeballing tourists.

A group of skinny Germans stand like telephone poles beside us. My peculiar scent does not go unnoticed.

One of the Germans asks, 'Why don't you go and shower? Better for everyone, no?'

This, I explain, is somewhat complicated. 'You see, we don't have any accommodation and all of our luggage is in Madrid.'

Madrid. A seven-hour bus ride away.

San Fermin, or the running of the bulls, was an unexpected addition to our travels. A hit-and-run mission poorly planned over a drunken late-night tapas session in a bar in a seedy suburb of Madrid.

Our grand plan involved talking our hostel owner into letting us store our backpacks behind reception for a night and booking return 24-hour bus tickets to Pamplona.

We would survive on a fistful of crumpled euros stuffed in our underwear and as much caffeine as our nervous systems could take.

THE NIGHT BEFORE...

Our first drink in Pamplona was in a clouded bar where cigar smoke smothered the roof as cigarette ash fell in small heaps on the stained wooden floor. The beer was served in thin plastic cups. If you took too long to drink, it warmed quickly in the dry summer air.

The giant town square was a sea of white and red as the sun slipped below the horizon and fireworks exploded among the early-rising stars. An eager mass of people walked around in crisp, white pants and shirts with thin red bandanas tied loosely around their necks. We bought pig skins filled with sangria in a discount supermarket and roamed the streets for hours.

Late in the evening, the pounding bass line from a bad 80s Spanish pop song drew yells of delight from the crowd at a bar on the outskirts of town. Hands went up and down to the music like their owners were throwing invisible balls in the air.

I was struggling to maintain a sitting position and contemplating mixing coffee with red wine, when Glen uttered words so ridiculous that he may as well have been arguing that the world was flat.

Punching my arm for attention, he said...

'HEY ISN'T THAT DENNIS RODMAN WALKING INTO THE BAR?'

A man whose basketball career had been plastered over my bedroom walls as a child. A man who stood 20-feet tall, dated the likes of Madonna and Carmen Electra, had a different hair colour for each day of the week and stained his flesh so many times with badly drawn tattoos that he would surely one day die of ink poisoning.

Three heavy-chested men parted the crowd on the dance floor and left a path for Rodman to approach the bar. The sneering bodyguards had arms like a python's belly, fat from a fresh kill, yet Rodman towered over them all.

I stood up in disbelief. I pushed past drunken, twisted bodies on the dance floor, trying to reach the bar and buy my new friend, Rodman, a drink.

I rustled around hastily in my underwear for a clean euro note.

A bodyguard barked something loud in Spanish, his spit spraying my face. He pushed hard against me, implying violence. I quickly learned a valuable lesson.

Do not try to approach a celebrity with a hand down the front of your pants.

BACK AT THE BULL RUN...

It's 7.45am, and I'm in a bad way. There is no way I can run. My face is a gangrenous green and covered in what I hope is just dried beer and mud.

People brave enough to run with the bulls jump a thick, wooden fence that separates them from the crowd of onlookers.

Glen stands on the road and gives me the middle finger. He's clearly not impressed with my self-restraint. He takes off his white t-shirt to reveal the yellow and brown stripes of a Hawthorn football jersey. He sticks his tongue out and asks if I can take his photo, in case he doesn't survive the bull run.

At 7.50am, a cannon explodes. The cavernous boom echoes off the surrounding buildings to signal that the bulls are coming. Spectators yell and throw half-empty glasses of wine in the air. My head feels like someone has embedded a large axe in my skull.

Nervous tourists begin sprinting long before the crashing hooves reach them. The locals hang back, waiting against the railings. They carry rolled-up magazines to smack the bulls on their arses as they run past.

A handful of petrified backpackers begin to have second thoughts about running. They jump at the fence, trying desperately to climb back over. The ground reverberates to the sound of a low, rolling thunder.

TIME SLOWS AND IT'S LIKE WATCHING A DARK, MOVING, VIOLENT POEM

A train of black, heaving muscle rumbles up the narrow, twisting road, ploughing spiked horns through anyone stupid enough to get in its way.

HALF A TANK OF CHARACTER

MELBOURNE, AUSTRALIA

Flies worship in numbers at the open bottle of BBQ sauce. The bread is hard from exposure to the afternoon sun; sausages cool on a blue Oscar the Grouch plastic plate.

Kirsty and Reagan walk past. They're fooling about like 14-year-olds at the movies, but swear there's nothing going on. I pinch Kirsty on the arm. She thinks it's Reagan. When she turns and smiles at him, I know she's a bad liar.

Someone asks if I can get off the esky, because they want a pale ale. I get my phone out to reply to a message that I got last night when we were at Honkytonks and I was too drunk to do anything about it.

I pretend not to notice as she walks over with her jeans rolled up above her ankles and asks, 'Do you want to leave? Get out of here soon?'

I ask Kirsty and Reagan if they'd like a lift. 'Do you guys need a ride, or are you just planning on rooting on the front lawn like you're cousins and we're living in Tasmania?'

Reagan punches me in the arm, but smiles.

'I don't know,' Kirsty says. 'I've been in the car with Paul before and don't really want to die.'

Reagan argues, 'We'll be fine. Anyway, it will be cheaper than a taxi.'

We say our goodbyes with kisses and rude gestures and walk to my off-green 1970s Toyota Corona. It sits two streets away, because we couldn't get a park closer without a permit.

We pile into my car with its off-key sound, worn-out sheepskin car seats, half a tank of character and obligatory 'Honk if you're horny' bumper sticker. A smile plays on Rolled Up Jeans's sunburnt lips.

She looks at me, eyes glazed over by a thin film of alcoholic idealism. Clutching her prized long-neck bottle of social lubricant, she says something that fills my heart to the brim.

'You know what's grouse?' Rolled Up Jeans suspends the question in mid-air, between mouthfuls of warm beer.

'What?' I ask, watching Kirsty and Reagan struggle in the back seat of the car, hands all over the place...

'BEING US.'

LOOK
THE
WHEN

ME IN
EYES
I POO

'Have I told you about my plant-based diet?' My friend asks, ordering a serving of chilli-cheese fries.

The waitress rolls her eyes and I look away, pretending I didn't hear a thing.

'Well,' Plant-based Dieter continues, 'It is more a conceptual approach to eating. It's a way of life. A plant-based diet is aspirational rather than something needing to be strictly adhered to.'

'No', I tell him, 'I'm pretty sure if you're on a plant-based diet, you eat only plant-based things.' What he is doing is eating anything he wants, including some vegetables that coincidently happen to be plants. It is less 'diet' and more 'annoying talking point.'

Our chilli-cheese fries arrive within minutes. The waitress reaches across the table to collect an empty glass. I notice a painful mural of tattoo ink on her left arm. There is a scrawling collection of seemingly unrelated images, from a train-track curling up her inner arm to what looks like a farmers' market stall on her shoulder.

Everyone in Brooklyn is inked. But we're not talking burly standover men with 'HATE' scrawled across their bruised knuckles. Here, you're more likely to be confronted at night by a malnourished, DIY-tattooed, bespectacled male looking for a late-evening lentil burger fix.

Brooklyn has changed. Street corners that once were home to drug dealers are now upcycled cafés selling cold-press coffee and organic pumpkin bread. Narrow laneways that once would have been ideal places to stash a corpse are now heaving with small late-night bars full of second-hand furniture and people retweeting 'Sad Kanye' memes.

Plant-based Dieter instructs me, 'We need a full meal before we go out drinking.' Ignoring the food he just consumed, he says, 'We should do American BBQ, unless you've had it recently?'

Most Australians' BBQ experiences consist of a flatulent uncle charring ground meat until it resembles a lump of coal as he sucks down warm beer and relays his borderline racist views of the new neighbours. Americans take BBQ a little more seriously.

We line up outside what used to be a vacant garage with a crowd of people waiting for a table at Fette Sau. Plant-based Dieter pushes to the front of the line. He has the false confidence of someone that used to possess a six-pack and take his shirt off on nightclub dance floor podiums for a handful of drink cards.

He asks how long it will take to get a table. The young man at the door frowns. Well, at least I think that's what he does. With barely any eyebrows, it's hard to tell. Our wait will be 45 minutes. I'm not that hungry, so we hail a yellow cab and head over the Williamsburg Bridge into Manhattan.

The taxi drops us in Chelsea, where another friend stands waiting. He is wearing a fluorescent-orange parachute jacket and looks like a giant, garish traffic safety cone.

Traffic Safety Cone waves. 'Hurry up! The guy on the door will finish his shift soon and that's the only way we're getting in,' he says.

The bar is vast, cavernous space. A DJ booth is suspended mid-air over a polished concrete dance floor.

We push through a conversation between a balding, middle-aged man in expensive loafers and a much younger athletic type, who has perfectly white teeth and wears a singlet top in New York in late January.

Traffic Safety Cone flirts with the guy behind the bar. Badly. He tries to get us a few free Long Island ice teas. Instead, we end up with three beers and no change from $20.

A dance remix of an early Madonna song drops, and the room erupts. Plant-based Dieter begins talking about his previous life as a semi-professional nightclub dancer.

'Professional seems like a pretty loose definition for someone who was only ever given drink cards for his efforts and not actually paid any money to dance,' I say.

'Really Paul? That's besides the point. I would have just spent the money on booze anyway,' Plant-based Dieter retorts.

I dance-walk my way to the back of the room, heading towards the bathroom. I push against the toilet door, take two steps inside and the world stops. Two eyeballs bore into my soul. Looking around the room I make eye contact with a large, hairy man.

He's sitting on a toilet that has no door. In fact, there is no cubicle at all. The male bathrooms are two urinals against a wall and a toilet sitting in the corner, mostly exposed.

THE HAIRY MAN STARES AT ME.

HE SITS THERE, EXPRESSIONLESS ... WATCHING. HE IS DEFIANT, PROUD AND DOING A SHIT IN FULL VIEW OF OTHER PEOPLE.

I freeze, unsure if I should turn away. Despite thinking of myself as progressive, I'm not entirely sure of the correct etiquette for this kind of situation. I want to turn and run, but also not offend anyone.

I slowly shuffle towards the stand-up urinal. The hairy man does not blink, his eyes fixed on mine. My heart pounds, fuelled by nervous energy. I stand at the urinal for two minutes, trying to ignore the shitting elephant in the room.

As much as I need to relieve myself, I simply cannot go. I zip myself up and, with a full bladder, make a swift exit. I push through the dance floor looking for my friends. I grab Traffic Safety Cone by the arm and tell him we need to leave.

Plant-based Dieter protests. 'Why should we go? I'm just starting to have a good time,' he says.

I rehash my bathroom disaster to a sceptical audience. Plant-based Dieter can't believe it. He wants to see for himself. Traffic Safety Cone laughs and tells me to loosen up.

'What?' I ask.

Traffic Safety Cone says, 'Don't worry. Relax. That guy is most likely just a local. With a particular fetish. He probably saves up his shits for the bar on a Saturday night. Sitting on the toilet, staring down anyone who comes into the bathroom. It sounds like a harmless reverse power play; a very niche fantasy being played out over an hour, or more.'

I shake my head in disbelief and insist we need to leave.

Traffic Safety Cone says, 'Don't be such a prude.'

Plant-based Dieter struggles to get his head around the situation. 'An hour to take a shit?' he asks. 'Surely not. Has he heard about the benefits of being a vegan?'

THE MOST EXPENSIVE TAXI IN MEXICO

13

PUERTO ESCONDIDO, MEXICO

A cloud of burning pig flesh hangs as a low, delicious fog over the slowly moving masses. The song of summer cicadas mixes in the air with the chatter of polite bartering, as a child sleeps on a straw mat beside his mother's market stall.

'Hurry up, we don't want to be late,' says Ivo. 'We told the German girls we would meet them after dinner. If we get there too late, we might miss our chance!'

A street band meanders down a paved laneway. The guitarists pick at their instruments with a lazy precision, a woman's voice serenades the passing crowd.

We push past a handful of locals dancing a clumsy ballet as the setting sun illuminates red-tiled rooftops in the beachside village of Puerto Escondido, Mexico.

We hurry through the street market, making our way to the beach. The last of the day's light plays on the thin stretch of sand, our footprints leave deep imprints with each passing step. Ivo pulls a neatly rolled joint out of his pocket.

'Just a little something I prepared earlier,' he says, fumbling around for a lighter.

The sky darkens, and the beach is empty. We walk along the shore towards Capa Blanca, the distinct smell of marijuana trailing behind us. Out of the dense, thick palm trees on the beach's edge comes a noise. Roaring. Terrifying.

I twist my head towards the ungodly man-made sound. An engine snarls.

A pick-up truck bursts out of the shadows heading towards us. Its tyres churn sand into the air like an apex predator ready for a kill.

Ivo and I freeze. The truck brakes abruptly. An explosion of sand is cast over our faces.

A spotlight blinds our eyes. Menacing voices instruct us not to move. Six large, heavily armed policemen jump from the back of the vehicle. One of them grabs my arm. His fingernails dig sharply into my shoulder, piercing the skin. We are pushed against the side of the truck. I hear Ivo's skull bounce against the metallic doorframe.

The driver barks an order at the other police. We are thrown face down into the back of the truck and gestures tell us not to say a word as we are driven away from town.

The truck moves slowly, silently, along the beach. The driver turns off the headlights. I look back to see Puerto Escondido become a hazy smudge of lights. After 15 minutes, the pick-up truck stops, and the police drag us from the vehicle.

I'm shoved back against the side of the truck and searched.

I WONDERED IF IT WAS TOO LATE TO COMPOSE A WILL.

An officer with a thick, 70s porn-star moustache pats Ivo down, instantly finding a bag of weed in his pocket. The marijuana is held high in the air. Voices rise. Another officer gestures wildly with a gun in his hand. The truck driver yells in Ivo's face. My arm is twisted behind my back as two more policemen draw their guns.

I see Ivo's face drained of all colour and wonder if this was the end. Ivo whispers, 'We should run.' 'Don't.' I say. 'There's no one around to stop them from using us as target practice.'

The truck driver pulls my hair and yells in my face. My throat tightens with fear. Finally, I mutter the only two words I know confidently in Spanish. '¿Quante questa?' Or, in English, 'How much?'

Their expressions change instantly. The policemen relax their grip on their guns and my arm is released from behind my back.

Officer Porn Star pulls out a pen and paper and writes down a number. He presents it to us like a sommelier trying to secure a table's approval for their wine recommendation. I shake my head at the first number. I gesture for the pen and write down a much smaller figure. Officer Porn Star makes a counteroffer.

After two minutes of negotiations, we settle on a figure that ensures our Mexican travel experience will not include a romantic overnight stay with a cellmate named Pedro.

'How much money do you have on you?' I ask Ivo. 'Not even close,' he replies.

I open my wallet and see that I only have a quarter of what we agreed to pay. The truck driver grabs my wallet out of my hand, pulls out my ATM card and smiles. He gestures for us to sit back in the truck.

We follow a dirt track leading us back into town. At the outskirts of Puerto Escondido, the truck slows to a stop. The driver tells us to get out, hands me the plastic fantastic and points to an ATM.

Reluctantly, I empty my bank account. We are now free to go.

'Fuck. That was all we had!' Ivo says. 'Now what are we going to do? And what about those German girls?'

We are broke. Our night is ruined. We have no money to buy drinks. No money to even get a taxi back to our side of town. We can't afford to get to Capa Blanca so that Ivo can begin his great Germanic love affair.

So, faced with a shortage of money and a limited grasp of what the proper social protocol is for behaving around recently bribed police, we take the only logical course of action presented to us.

'Follow my lead, I've got a plan,' I tell Ivo.

The police are not pleased to see us again. Officer Porn Star shouts in my face, another reaches for his gun. I hold my hands up, gesturing for everyone to relax. In broken Spanish and uncoordinated hand gestures, I try to explain that all we want is a lift. 'You... drive... us... Capa Blanca...'

The truck driver laughs. He talks quickly to the other members of his team. Their faces relax. An officer places a meaty palm on my shoulder. He gestures for us to jump back up into the truck.

The policemen laugh with Ivo and I as we drive down the side streets of Puerto Escondido. The early evening air is warm, even at speed. Our truck moves to the wrong side of the road. The police truck muscles between vehicles and we watch as pedestrians jump out of its way.

There is a long line outside Capa Blanca. A board outside the club advertises a cover charge higher than our zero-dollar bank balances will cover.

Some people turn heads by arriving at a nightclub entrance in fancy sports cars, models on their arms and dripping in gold chains. But from personal experience, I can confirm that if you really want to get noticed (and get club security on side)...

PULLING UP IN A PICK-UP TRUCK **FULL OF HEAVILY ARMED POLICE OFFICERS WORKS A CHARM.**

A THING OF SAVAGE BEAUTY

14

SAN PEDRO LA LAGUNA, GUATEMALA

The sky is dark, coloured like a deep, fresh bruise. A feral wind thrashes across the broken surface of the lake, pushing water deep onto the shore. A thin, twisting branch of lightning shatters on the horizon. The surrounding mountains are lit for a brief second: their silhouettes loom large over the tiny villages at the water's edge. The vast lake is a violent, shadowy broth and our small wooden boat doesn't stand a chance.

The boat is silent with panic. There are no life jackets, no flares to signal for help. Tourists sit on top of backpacks and clutch their worn, dog-eared phrase books like they were bibles. Local Guatemalans cross themselves and mutter prayers under their breath. There are too many people on the boat. The bow barely sits above the moving bulk of water and threatens to go under the larger waves.

The wind carries water from the lake at speed. It drives into the side of my face, stinging the exposed skin. I see our boat's captain try to stand up. He flashes a light towards the distant village of Panajachel but doesn't get any response.

We are the only boat on Lake Atitlán. Every passenger is alone with their fear.

The engine belches up a smoky, burnt cloud of petrol. The motor is weak and barely audible above the storm. The Captain frantically positions the boat to face a coming wave. We ride the crest and continue a slow, painful crossing to our destination of San Pedro La Laguna.

It takes the better part of an hour, but our boat eventually pulls alongside a slowly rotting dock. The wood of the dock bends and sinks when luggage is hauled onto it.

The Captain sits in a broken heap over the engine. A thick greasy film of sweat coats his face. His empty, beaten expression and eyes that won't stop blinking tell me that there will be no other lake crossings today.

Fat droplets of rain blow through the town of San Pedro. A handful of locals surround Drew and I as we get off the boat. They carry dirty, laminated sheets of paper with maps of the town and photos of empty beds. We have nowhere to stay and walk away with a tanned man whose hostel is close to the dock.

Drew and I struggle up a stony path. My soaked clothes stick to my body like a weighty second skin. We drop our backpacks at the hostel entrance. They splash thin, watery mud across the tiled floor. The hostel owner flashes a set of yellow teeth.

'You had a big adventure on the lake,' he says. 'Go shower and lie down. Check-in later.'

The hostel dorm room smells like stale beer and tobacco. The walls are painted dark green. Our flesh looks gangrenous under the naked light bulb.

I fall onto a hard mattress. My eyelids barely meet before the bathroom explodes with shouted profanities.

'Stupid fucking shit of a thing.'

Drew has cut himself on broken glass. He tracks bloodied footprints across the room, asking for help.

I notice a shadow moving silently across the green ceiling. Something is shuffling towards the light. The shadow is as big as a small child's torso. I see that it has eight thick, hairy legs.

My heart pounds. I open my mouth. I'm desperate to yell 'Tarantula!', but can only make a weak, broken noise like a dying crow's last squawk. My brain sends frantic signals to my limbs, instructing them to shift. I roll off the bed in wild panic. I shout hysterically,

Drew catches sight of the giant shadow. In a few short seconds, we are sprinting down the rocky path outside the hostel. Our bags and belongings falling in a trail of chaos behind us. No one speaks. We run a kilometre across town for no reason, only to empty ourselves of fear.

I vow to never return to the green hostel, the home of giant man-eating spiders. We settle on a new home that overlooks the village of San Pedro and shine our torches under every bed before we fall asleep.

The next morning, I wake to sunshine coming through an open window. The view from our room takes in a wide, tree-fringed view of the lake. The lake is a thing of savage beauty, framed by jagged mountain peaks and volcanic craters. After breakfast, Drew and I walk to the lake's edge. We swim out into the darkness of the deeper water.

Our friend from Andorra, Luis, tells us an alarming story.

'I went to buy some cigarettes after breakfast. The shopkeeper told me that the chicken bus from Guatemala City to Panajachel was hijacked a week ago. This was the same bus route we rode yesterday,' he says.

'Apparently masked gunmen boarded the bus and stripped passengers of money, watches and mobile phones. The bus driver was beaten. His jaw is now held together by thin metal wires. All of this because there were no tourists on the bus. There was nobody worth holding for ransom.'

Late in the afternoon, the three of us set off on a hike. We push through the dense foliage at the base of Volcán San Pedro. It isn't long before my bloody footed friend complains that we should turn back.

The hiking trail twists around a fallen boulder. On the other side, we meet an old man. He wears a dirty, ripped football shirt and walks barefoot over rocks. There is pain in his eyes. He holds Luis for support. The old man begins talking in a high-pitched tone, almost a cry.

Luis translates, 'The old man comes from a village a few kilometres away. Half of the village was destroyed in a massive mudslide over two nights ago. Some of his family are missing. He has no home, no food and no water to help those that are still around.'

The old man has tears running down creased cheeks. 'He is asking us for help,' Luis says. 'Unless he can get food, water and some money to help his family through the next few days, he will be forced to come into San Pedro and rob a tourist.'

The old man is bent over and looking at the ground. We dig around for our wallets. I reach into my backpack and hand over a crumpled, sweaty fistful of quetzals and US dollars.

The setting sun breaks through a thick bank of clouds. Splinters of fleeting daylight touch the hiking trail. I feel heavy on my feet.

The old man folds the money for his family into a dirty pocket. He clutches our hands tightly and doesn't say another word.

The first stars of the evening emerge above us. The old man turns slowly. He walks a winding path away from town with a rusted machete hanging loosely from a rope belt.

DARK CIRCLES RIMMING BLOODSHOT EYES

15

BUENOS AIRES, ARGENTINA

Ice melts in a glass. Dark circles rim my bloodshot eyes. A look at my watch tells me it is 6pm on a Monday evening in Melbourne. Which would be fine, except that I'm in a nightclub in Buenos Aires and the day hasn't even started.

A skinny man shakes an empty drink in the air trying to motivate the girl behind the bar. She casts a bored look in my direction. I catch myself yawning. It has been a long night.

The last time my head touched anything resembling a pillow was a rolled-up leather jacket on an economy flight from Australia. I don't know where my friends are. I can't remember the last time I lay in a bed.

Like a scene from a bad 80s film clip (big on hair-sprayed manes and smoke machines), a friend emerges from the hazy masses. His Justin Bieber-inspired fringe is a greasy mess on his forehead. It is about time he got a more age-appropriate haircut. It is also about time that we found Jake and admit that Buenos Aires has destroyed us on our first night in the city.

Jake has been missing for hours. As the only single man in our party of three, he has worked overtime chasing anything with at least shoulder-length hair and no visible Adam's apple. Perhaps we'll see him on the news as one of those tourists who goes home with a local and wakes up in a bath full of ice with a kidney missing. Good luck explaining that one to your mother via email.

Half a lap around the nightclub later, we discover Jake inflicting crimes against dance and coordinated body movement in front of some poor unsuspecting local. Meanwhile, I can barely walk.

I croak that Bieber-Inspired Fringe and I are leaving. Jake can't speak Spanish but suspects the girl is keen on him because she has not run away yet.

Bieber-Inspired Fringe and I move towards the exit. Passing a mirror, I see a pair of zombies. The bouncer looks happy to see us leave.

The early morning sun is a blinding force of light. A taxi pulls up and Bieber-Inspired fringe and I fall inside. Jake jumps in at the last minute. Solo. Clutching a piece of paper.

'What happened with the local?', I ask. Jake waves a set of scribbled numbers in front of us with a cheesy grin. 'Digits,' he says proudly.

'That doesn't make sense,' Bieber-Inspired Fringe says. 'What good is a phone number when you can't speak Spanish?'

Our hostel is eerily quiet. There is no one around bar a few other nocturnal latecomers struggling up the stairs.

The girl at reception laughs and says, 'No one comes to Buenos Aires to eat breakfast.'

SLEEP DOES NOT COME EASY.

The bed is narrow and hard, light comes in from an open window and my body clock wages war with my mind.

I wake late in the day with a thumping headache. A cool, late afternoon breeze blows across the rooftops.

I walk up a set of aged wooden stairs and look out over the city.

A young woman with mousy brown hair and thick-rimmed glasses comes around the corner. She could easily be the type to frequent an art gallery specialising in Che Guevara motifs or a restaurant with a lentil-focused menu. In a thick French accent, she asks:

'Are you Craig?'

A table across from me splutters to life. Its resident coughs up a lung and swears, then draws the life out a cigarette held tightly between his fingers.

'I'm Craig,' he says, looking 10 years older than he probably is. His voice sounds like he has been gargling gravel for the last two hours. There are bags under his eyes and his skin looks washed out.

The streets below our hostel hum with the sounds of peak hour. The sun finally disappears below the Buenos Aires skyline as I crack my first beer. It is a Monday night. An evening usually spent recovering from the first day of the working week. An evening made for imported American TV sitcoms and going to bed early.

Craig tells anyone who will listen that there is a warehouse party happening in the city's north, and asks if we want to come along.

Two trains and 45 minutes later, we arrive in Abasto. It is the type of suburb where people walk slower and smoke hand-rolled cigarettes.

A group of university students sell cheap alcohol from the roadside. The first mouthful is like swallowing petrol, or hospital-grade disinfectant.

There is a 100-metre line leading up to the warehouse.

Graffiti covers the walls of the industrial park. Not loose, obnoxious tagging, but sprawling, wall-covering murals that look like painful tattoos on the factory's skin.

A huge cheer goes up from inside the warehouse as the stage is swarmed by a group of musicians. There must be over a thousand people at this party, all shunning early bedtimes and imported TV. Jake, Bieber-Inspired fringe and I move towards the centre of the dance floor and are engulfed by the sounds of 17 percussionists setting a frenetic beat.

Jake goes off in search of another girl with shoulder-length hair and no visible Adam's apple.

Bieber-Inspired Fringe and I try to push our way to the front of the crowd. Around us university students, office workers, artists and fellow tourists are squeezing the life out of their Monday evening.

At a break in the music, I go looking for a drink. The makeshift bar has a lengthy queue. When I get to the front of the line, I am surprised to hear the girl pouring my vodka has an English accent.

She tells me she came to the city on a student exchange, 'But I've outstayed my visa and now survive by making cash by selling marked-up alcohol at local events.'

I ask her if she knows the next group of musicians. I ask her if they will be any good.

She laughs, tells me not to be stupid. 'This is Buenos Aires after the sun's gone down. It's all good.'

EXIT

THE SC

16

ELGOIBAR, SPAIN

CIETY

Sunset steals into the kitchen. It has been raining again. The horizon is smudged grey and orange as if someone has smeared a dirty thumb along where land ends and the sky should begin. Ramon weighs a bulb of garlic in one hand. He pushes away a half glass of cider. An old digital clock flashes neon red from across the room.

'They're always late,' Ramon sighs.

We walk outside. The main road steams as an overladen truck, pregnant with dairy for the market, passes at speed.

A sign above the bus stop indicates that we are in Elgoibar, Basque Country, northern Spain. The town pays homage to the functionality of concrete. Stark, drab, rectangular apartment blocks jut out of the ground. The shades of residential grey are punctuated by painted maps hanging across apartment balconies. The maps are an outline of Basque Country, emblazoned with large red arrows.

I point out the maps and ask Ramon 'What's all this about?'

In his deep, commanding voice, Ramon says, 'When people are arrested for being members of Basque's separatist group ETA, or suspected of carrying out activities in its support, they are sent to jails in the Spanish colonies in Africa.

'The maps with the red arrows are a message: "Bring our sons, daughters, brothers and sisters home. Jail them if they are guilty, but let their families visit... don't isolate them a world away".'

It is said that the Basque language is the oldest in Western Europe, and that their people are the oldest permanent residents of the continent. The pocket of northern Spain and southern France that they occupy is cruel in its beauty. It leaves you wondering how you got cheated out of such natural scenery when you were growing up.

The thick green forests, untouched by water restrictions, soaring mountains and isolated farmhouses of Basque Country lampoon the sprawling suburbia and flat, brown expanses of my youth on the peripheries of Melbourne.

Ramon is back in the kitchen with a knife in his hand. Flashes of silver dance across the blade under a naked light bulb. It cuts smoothly into the flesh of a tuna.

'This dish is better prepared one day in advance,' Ramon says.

I ask, 'Is it a traditional Spanish recipe?'

Ramon puts the knife down. He tells me to be careful.

'THE BASQUES ARE PROUD. DON'T CALL THEIR FOOD SPANISH.'

Ramon picks up a bruised tomato and squeezes until it explodes over a pot of half-cooked onions. He says, 'Last century the Basques were brutally oppressed by the Spanish dictator, General Franco. The Basque culture, our language and our way of life were to be stamped out.'

Ramon's family only learned Basque through being taught by older relatives and family friends in isolated farmhouses. If they were caught, those passing on their native tongue would have had a four-walled cell from which to contemplate their passion for education.

Thick chunks of tuna fall into a crimson sea of softened red peppers. Ramon takes care to wipe the bench clean of splash marks, like he is polishing a car for his daughter's wedding. There is a mound of rough, earthy potatoes waiting to be guillotined on a wooden chopping board and it's clear that there's more work to be done.

Perhaps more than anywhere else in Europe, Basques are obsessed with food. Since the 1870s, Basque men have been secretly gathering in small member-based groups and cooking together in communal kitchens called *txokos*, or societies.

There's a knock at the front door. The echo of bare knuckles against stained wood announces the arrival of Ramon's family. He rests a worn wooden spoon on a pillow of soft-boiled potatoes. Voices come running into the room, followed by the people they belong to. A tsunami of chatter; the six people fill the large room. The kitchen is quickly occupied by shaved cured hams, local hard cheese and juicy peaches.

Ramon kisses everyone twice, then waves them away. A growing mist engulfs the kitchen as a pot comes to boil. Ramon turns the heat down.

Ramon clears his throat. 'During the Franco years, txokos filled the stomachs of the Basque people and became venues of defiance,' he explains. 'They were one of the only places where Basques could legally meet without state control.'

A PLACE WHERE THEY COULD SPEAK BASQUE, SING BASQUE AND BE BASQUE.

Ramon's wife is in the kitchen telling a story about a cousin who can't find work. It seems to be a story told many times in these parts. More than half of people under the age of 35 are out of work.

I ask Ramon, 'What is this doing to the country?'

Ramon doesn't say a thing. He just points a twisted finger, scarred by the cuts and callouses of someone who relies on his hands for a living, to his temple and twists like he is opening a new bottle of wine.

The family binds around a thick wooden table. Bread is ripped from a long cob and placed beside shallow bowls.

Ramon struggles under the weight of a giant pot full of *marmitako*, the fish stew he was preparing earlier.

I say to Ramon, 'I've hardly seen a fast-food chain since I came to Basque Country.' He smiles, and deep lines carve into his cheeks.

'They will never work. People here like to know who they are buying their food from, where it comes from,' Ramon says.

Ramon arches his neck back so that his eyes follow the cracks in the plaster roof. His wife wraps an arm around his waist. The table explodes in laughter as the grandmother's glasses fog from the steam of the freshly served marmitako.

17

THE ANIMAL IS MANIC

ARCTIC CIRCLE, NORWAY

Darkness rises. A chunky, Scandinavian man-mountain stands in front of me. He has a ginger afro and a 'Not allowed within 200 metres of a primary school' feel about him.

He tells me to take off my clothes.

Apparently, I have not come prepared for winter in the Arctic Circle. My Adidas cross trainers and black skinny jeans are as inappropriate for the conditions as a second-hand pair of Speedos at a funeral. I walk into a sweaty wooden chamber; a handful of people remove their pants in front of me.

HAIRY BALL-SACKS AND REINDEER ANTLERS.

It is impossible to walk into a room in Norway and not see at least one of these things. Norway is a country largely populated by beautiful giants. Norwegians look like they spend their evenings dozing in seal-placenta facemasks, before waking to a daily routine of hot yoga and looking fabulously uninterested while scaling an ice cliff.

I am given snowshoes, Gore-Tex pants and a jacket that is two-inches thick. It is a struggle to change clothes and maintain any form of dignity. I literally fall out of the change room, grunting aggressively while trying to pull the waterproof material over my thighs. Eventually I admit defeat and get dressed on a wooden bench in the hallway. The overhang of my beer belly is in full view of an elderly Japanese couple who whisper to each other and try to avert their eyes.

Outside, the sun is no longer visible. It is 2pm. A chilling wind wails. The air temperature is -8°C.

Ice cracks. Thin metal spikes on the soles of my new shoes pierce the roadside winter covering. A dog howls in the distance, another snarls.

'Come and meet your engine room,' Man Mountain tells me cheerily.

A pack of world-weary husky dogs bark as we approach. The snow underneath them is piss-yellow.

'Ever driven a dog sled before?' asks Man Mountain, like it was a 50/50 proposition that I had.

We unchain half-a-dozen dogs from their kennels and attach them to harnesses in front of a wooden sled. Man Mountain gives me a two-minute crash-course in how to drive.

'You need to lean into the corners. Brake if you are going too fast and – whatever you do – stick to the path. The dogs know what they are doing, so really all you need to do is pay attention and just...'

Don't.

Fuck.

It.

Up.

Before we set off, Man Mountain waves to a local fisherman walking towards the harbour. The fisherman nods and cups a cigarette with his fingers. The smoke from his hand-rolled cigarette billows from his mouth like the exhaust of a factory. He might be preparing to go out to sea in gale-force winds, but he equally could have been off to watch a lawn-bowls tournament for all that his expression gives away.

He stamps out his cigarette and unfolds a stick of chewing gum. He looks like the idea of freezing to death, alone in a violent ocean, would only bore him.

Four dog sleds move ahead of me. Man Mountain holds me back. 'The older animals at the back of your sled will set the pace,' he tells me. 'Remember to stamp on the metal brake ahead of turning. Too much speed and the sled will flip.'

The sled lurches forward and I grip the reins. We are the last to move in our group on this 45-minute journey to a collection of ice huts over the horizon. The dogs pull and bark in excitement, seemingly happy to be running the semi-worn snow path.

We quickly catch the sled in front. I stamp down on the brake to avoid a collision. The dogs respond by pulling harder, but the resistance of a metal plate digging into the snow slows our momentum.

A sudden wind whips across the frozen surface of a nearby lake, slapping me in the face. I turn to shield myself from the wind. Ice collects in frozen droplets on the naked branches of hibernating trees. I slow my dogs and the other sleds disappear out of vision.

The Arctic Circle really does look different to anywhere else. A vast white vista broken only by the dark of the sky.

The sled follows a twisting path. We gain speed downhill, trying to catch up with those in front. The Man Mountain is nowhere to be seen.

One of the dogs turns its head, catching my eye.

THE ANIMAL LOOKS MANIC...

Possibly psychotic. I make a mental note to avoid it like a racist uncle's Facebook friend request.

We come to a steep corner and I brake late – too late. The dogs are pulling too fast and I cannot stop. The sled hits a snow wall with violence and I launch into the air.

My face is pushed into the snow. The dog harness becomes untethered. The sled falls over my legs. I can't breathe.

The dogs run free into the distance. I roll onto my back and the air is suddenly still. Thin. Like there is not enough to go around.

MIDNIGHT IN STAB CITY

18 LONDON, ENGLAND

The night is bitter. Freezing. A thick London fog chokes the city, cutting visibility to under 10 metres. Several boys from the local housing estate stand around the edge of a park kicking a football . They stare down the passers-by that stumble down their lane.

A faint red hue spills out from the window of a packed cocktail bar and the light is reflected in the dirty water running along the gutter.

I motion for us to head in out of the cold. I can't feel my face. Bryce shakes his head, saying 'We're nearly there.'

I used to live in London and there are some important lessons I will never forget:

- Don't ever visit a dentist in the UK unless you really must or want to end up with a misshaped mouth that will make people question whether your physical deficiencies are a result of centuries of inbreeding
- Don't bother trying to smell nice after catching the Tube in the middle of summer and,
- Don't, under any circumstances, be out in East London after midnight, unless you have a death wish, or are so enamoured with acupuncture that you're willing to let a teenager poke you with a blunt knife for the contents of your wallet.

I remember reading a BBC story which compared crime rates in the East London suburb of Hackney with other murder hot spots around the world such as Johannesburg and Sao Paulo.

The article called East London the 'Stabbing capital of the UK.' It painted the picture of the last place you'd want to be after dark.

Mr Brown asks Bryce, 'What time is it and where are we exactly? I have no fucking idea on either account.'

Bryce pulls his collar up to shield against the cold. He shoves his hands into his pockets.

'It is after midnight and we're in Shoreditch, East London,' he replies.

I cough nervously. My testicles disappear up into my chest. Glancing around me, though, I start to register that many things have changed in the years since I lived in London.

In that time, I have gotten older, my hangovers have gotten more severe and East London has gone from 'Murder City' to become the European epicentre of skinny jeans, fixie bikes and ironic beards.

'We're here,' Bryce says, pointing a bony finger at a casual late-night diner across the street.

I look suspiciously through the window. I was promised late-night debauchery, hard liquor and feeling like death the next morning.

The place Bryce has led us to looks too sanitised. A family of tourists with children in matching red jackets enjoy a round of milkshakes. It doesn't look like a bar at all.

WHAT KIND OF DEMENTED HELL HAVE YOU LED US TO?

'It looks like a shit McDonald's,' Mr Brown remarks. Mr Brown lives on a houseboat and doesn't think there is anything unusual about it.

Bryce flashes the type of straight-toothed smile that proves he has not yet visited a local dentist.

'Don't worry,' he says. 'Just follow my lead and walk towards the toilets.'

We push past tables filled with friends and families picking over meals and indulging in casual conversation. The bathroom door swings open and a mother shepherds a child past us. She eyes our group huddled into the bathroom passageway with suspicion. I feel the sudden urge to blurt out that we're not here for a gang bang, just looking for a place to drink.

There are three doors in the passageway: one with the outline of the female form, one with a male outline and one with a security pin code lock. Thick scrawls of white chalk scream 'Private!' across the dark green paint of the security coded door.

To my surprise, Bryce pushes his thin, pale wrists against the 'Private' door hesitantly, like he is poking a hibernating grizzly bear in the soft flesh of its belly just to see what happens. The door opens with ease.

We walk lightly down a dimly lit passageway. I steal a look over my shoulder, half expecting to be chased out by a staff member demanding to know how the hell we got past their foolproof security door.

At the end of the passageway there is a thick metal door. Bryce holds it open and we walk outside and down two flights of fire-escape stairs. There is nothing at the bottom of the stairs except for stained concrete, small piles of rubbish and another thick, unmarked door.

The unmarked door opens.

My eyes frantically pivot around the room beyond. Towering columns of liquor stand tall against a mirrored wall. The whole room resembles a decadent 1920s brothel.

A man behind the bar finely slices a cucumber and heavy-handedly pours gin.

He waves his head, gesturing us to a table at the far end of the room.

The speakeasy bar's menu is a roll call of classic cocktails and specialty, imported alcohols that could as easily strip paint from walls or dissolve a dead body as get you drunk. The vast space is all Prohibition-era glamour, with period wallpaper, drinking booths, a massive old bank vault and a bar complete with brass fittings. The room is full of people serious about their drinking and conversation.

A skinny, middle-aged waiter sporting an even skinnier waxed moustache walks straight-limbed over to our table. His black jeans are so tight that I'm sure I can see the veins on his legs throbbing every time he moves a foot. He pours chilled water from a jug into three frosted glasses.

The waiter asks, 'So gents, what'll be your poison?'

A thick cocktail menu is passed around the table and I ask for a 'Stabby Sally' (apparently an old East London cocktail). The waiter smiles and his moustache is crooked on his face.

I ask him what the drink is like. He laughs and says,

'LIKE A KNIFE TO THE GUT.'

MADNESS GROWS AROUND ME

19

BUENOS AIRES, ARGENTINA

A large white van pulls up by the roadside. Tires bald. Windows tinted. Anonymous. People go missing every day in Argentina. They have their bank balances cleared and are never seen again. The doors open and a balding man with a broken nose jumps out. He twitches. Sucks the life out of a cigarette.

'Get in,' Broken Nose tells us.

No one would even know we were gone.

Broken Nose looks like a badly sketched version of a South American con artist, or worse. His voice is scratchy and all over the place. His eyes look like a road map with streets and highways snaking out from his pupils in red.

'Sorry for the way I look today. Bit of a big one last night,' says Broken Nose. He opens a bottle of Coke, smiles and tells us 'It's time for breakfast.'

My watch tells me it is 3pm.

A portly Canadian sits at the back of the van. His words twang upwards at the end.

'Why do we have to leave so early for the match? Kick-off isn't until 6pm?' Portly Canadian whines.

Broken Nose throws his cigarette out of the window. He turns around in his chair and says 'You can't just turn up to the match 10 minutes before it starts. There are rules that must be followed'.

Portly Canadian doesn't know when to give up. 'What's the worst that could happen?' he asks.

Broken Nose snarls. A hint of sadistic glee lights up his face. He says three words. 'You. Could. Die.'

Portly Canadian looks like he is trying to suppress a painful fart. Broken Nose turns back in his seat and smiles loosely, enjoying the words that have stumbled out of his mouth.

He wasn't lying. Since Argentine football turned professional in 1931, roughly 250 people have died as a direct result of football-related violence. Two-hundred-and-fifty people in the wrong place. At the wrong time. In the wrong team colours.

We drive towards La Boca. Our van passes through streets marked with potholes and framed with crumbling buildings. Graffiti is everywhere.

A group of young boys kick a football down a side street, laughing carelessly. Broken Nose tells us to never come here on our own.

From the wrong side of town, Boca Juniors are the working man's club, where the poor come from off the street to get rich off 90 minutes of athletic theatre. Don't let their humble origins fool you, Boca Juniors don't beg, steal or hijack matches. They have some 50 titles to their name, they have the history and they have the players. They have a home ground that I've been told is a cauldron of madness and the backdrop to sporting fine art.

We near the stadium and our van is consumed by a heaving mass of slow-moving people. The road moves like we are stuck behind a conga line of geriatrics. The masses wear blue and yellow. Trumpets go off in the street.

Our vehicle inches forward – and then not at all. The doors open and the trumpets become louder. Piercing.

We are told, 'Get out. But stay together.' We walk to a police check, where we are all patted down. Thoroughly. It's pleasant enough, but I leave feeling cheap. Used. I wonder if I should leave a tip.

We enter the stadium. Concrete seats spill down in front of us to the edge of the football pitch. The best seats look taken, but there are five rows at the very front that are free. They stand clear in the sunshine, unobstructed from the extra tier of seats above us.

We move towards the prize seats. Broken Nose laughs. He shakes his head. He asks us why we think the seats are free. He explains that those seats aren't covered by the tier of seating above us. Above us is the opposition seating.

'What will the opposition fans do?' I ask. 'Throw food at us? Spit on us?'

'No,' the Broken Nose says.

'You will get pissed on.'

The teams of Boca Junior and Tigre come out on the ground to warm up. The stand shakes with noise and violent anticipation. The whistle for kick-off has to come soon or I fear the local standing next to me may spontaneously combust.

HE SCREAMS FOR BOCA. HE HOLDS HIS HANDS IN PRAYER. HE IS ANYTHING BUT AT PEACE.

A loudspeaker spits out feedback. It crackles and screeches before coming to life. Each player is announced to a primal roar from the adoring masses.

At the opposite end of the stadium stand Boca Junior's hardcore fan base. They are a crazed throng of convulsing bodies. They thrash the air. Scream. Bang drums. A huge banner is unfurled. The sound of a full brass band starts up from nowhere. A chant echoes across the stands.

The madness grows around me.

Another group of tourists arrive late and see the seats at the front of the stadium. They scramble to take them. The locals laugh. Broken Nose raises his eyebrows.

The match kicks off.

The hardcore fans surge towards a wire fence at the edge of the pitch. They riot against the chain-link. Bodies slam into each other as they empty their lungs screaming for a Boca victory.

In front of me, a young boy climbs the wire fence. He holds up a Boca flag. He shouts insults at the opposition fans above us.

The game builds up slowly.

With the patience of Zen masters, Boca's famed midfielders take their time in choosing their passes, dictating the play. The ball moves from end to end. When a goal is finally scored by Boca, the stadium erupts in nuclear celebration.

I see a steady stream of liquid rain down from above us onto the prime seats up front. The tourists look up in horror. Their faces look pained. Violated. Scarred by the foul liquid sprayed from above.

Half-time sees my bladder questioning the pre-match beers.

I want to go to the toilet but remember a friend's warning. They had recently been to a game and attempted to use the toilet. They walked into the bathroom with a full bladder and left minus a wallet.

On the plus side, the red mark left by the knife held to their throat didn't take long to fade.

I cross my legs and hope for no extra time.

The second half is a frenetic blur. First, the Tigre opposition tear up the script. They score twice, outplaying Boca and silencing the fans. Then, like a wounded beast who realises the spear in their side is actually a toothpick, Boca comes snarling back to life. The fans eject a thunderous roar when the yellow-and-blue slam the ball into the back of the net – twice – to take the lead.

The closing minutes of the match are dulled by a late equaliser from Tigre. The final whistle goes. A three-all draw. I feel flat.

The Tigre fans have taken the draw like a victory. They slam their feet into the stadium stairs, yelling like wild men.

Drunk off adrenaline and the raw emotion of the contest, I turn to slowly make my way to the exit. I'm surprised to see the stairs down from the stadium are completely blocked off. We are stuck, with no way out. Broken Nose tells us to come back and get comfortable. We're not going anywhere.

The Tigre fans chant as they leave the stadium. They throw insults over their shoulders. A growing number of Boca fans smash their fists against the gate holding us in.

We will have to wait an hour in the stadium for the Tigre fans to leave the area. I ask Broken Nose, 'Why can't we leave? Why do we have to wait around for so long?'

'It's only fair,' he replies.

'What's fair?' I ask.

Broken Nose's lips curl up at the sides. I've seen this look before. He winks and says,

'IT'S ONLY FAIR WE GIVE THEM A HEAD START.'

MAN VERSUS GPS

20

ASTURIAS, SPAIN

A faint, sickle-shaped moon hangs low in the sky. Barely illuminating. The evening is coming to its darkest hour. There are no other cars on the road. No other lights. No other people.

A ghostly shadow passes in front of our headlights. I suppress the urge to vomit and taste fear. We seem to have unwittingly stumbled onto the set of our own horror movie. I keep expecting our car to break down, a friendly local to stop to help, while I remark how curious it is that he needed to bring a chainsaw over to help get us started.

It wasn't supposed to be like this. We should be there by now.

The car erupts in an explosion of angry voices. Maria yells at Ramon, who is driving the car. Her mother, Rosa, joins in, until Ramon is surrounded by furious words and hands making obscene gestures.

To be honest, Ramon only has himself to blame. Some hours ago, as we were driving through the Cantabrian mountains in the Asturias region of northern Spain, a small electronic voice interrupted our conversation. 'Stay on your current road for three kilometres,' it said.

We were stopped at an intersection. Ramon had never been on these roads before, but insisted he knew what he was doing.

'The GPS must have it wrong,' he grumbled as he turned the navigation equipment off.

Leaving the main road, Ramon opted for a smaller path that twisted ominously up a mountain. 'This must be a quicker way,' he said.

Now, the car is quiet as Maria and Rosa draw breath. The windows are steamed over by the heat of the previous verbal onslaught.

Ramon finally admits defeat. The GPS is switched back on.

We are greeted with a repeated message, 'Wrong way. Wrong way. Turn around and follow the road 20 kilometres back to an intersection.'

Our car makes a wide turn. We face the direction we came from and begin to drive in tense silence.

We eventually reach a large town called Llanes. The streets look empty, like a plague has recently passed through. We stop several times to ask for directions to our house, but no one has heard of the street we are supposed to be staying in.

I KNOW ENOUGH SPANISH TO UNDERSTAND ROSA SWEARING UNDER HER BREATH.

The next morning all is forgiven. Opening the windows, I am presented with a clean, blue sky. My eyes salivate. The mountains of the Asturias stand proudly in the early morning air.

We are in a national park called Picos de Europa (the 'Peaks of Europe'), a mountain range that earned its name as the first sight of Europe for ships arriving from the Americas.

Rising above all other mountains in the range, like a professional basketball player in a jockey group photo, is the Naranjo de Bulnes. At over 2500 metres high, the mountain demands respect. Its presence will follow us everywhere we go in the region.

Getting lost today is optional. We don't have anywhere to be, no time to be there, so we just drive. Hillside villages come and go. We stop in one for an early lunch that is heavy on pungent cheese.

After lunch, we drive through a mountain pass. The view would be amazing if not for my fear of death distracting me as a small truck tries to pass us on the other side of the road.

We reach a tiny, stone-built mountain village with no name. We stretch and begin a slow walk through the narrow streets.

The locals smile at us as they go about their day. An old lady laughs when we try to take a photo outside the local church. 'Don't bother. It's falling down,' she says.

Our afternoon passes quickly as we walk along a mountain trail and stumble upon a number of small villages. Each has its own group of friendly locals and collection of cheeses that should be quarantined.

By the time we drive back into Llanes for dinner, the sun has slipped behind the mountains. Its last burst of light paints the sky a pale orange.

Walking into the restaurant, my lungs are assaulted by a thick haze of cigar smoke. We have come to a place where the locals eat – national smoking laws be damned.

The restaurant is loud. My Spanish is embarrassing.

'What do you want to eat?' The waiter asks me. I gesture that I will have the same as Ramon.

Ramon nods in agreement, says something I cannot understand to the waiter and they share a laugh. I think I may have made a mistake.

Our meals arrive after a number of beers. A great slab of wood is pulled over next to our table. On top of the slab is a gigantic hunk of blood-oozing beef. It is the size of a small pony.

The waiter comes to our table trying to put a cheese sauce on my plate. I stab at him wildly with a bloodied fork until he runs away.

I barely make a dent in the recently carved corpse before I feel like a heart attack is only a mouthful away.

Later that night, sleep does not come easy. I stare at the ceiling and nurse my swollen belly.

Eventually the morning comes, and I go in search of something stronger than aspirin. Outside the air is crisp, clear. The view is framed with the soaring peaks of the distant mountain range.

We pack up the farmhouse and return the keys to a local. He isn't the landlord, he says, 'But I know him well and will give him the keys when I see him next.'

That's how things are done in this part of Spain: simply, honestly and as part of a community.

We decide the time has come to head back to Basque Country and get back in the car. It's a long drive, but at least this time the roads will be familiar. At least this time, we will know the way.

From the back seat, I see Ramon reach over to the GPS on the dashboard.

An electronic voice starts up, says, 'Take the second left at the upcoming intersection.'

Ramon nods his head obediently and we begin to drive.

MEET ME IN THE BONG ROOM

21 LONDON, ENGLAND

Thanks to the cunt who
left the freezer door open
last night. Now my ice-cream
is melted and the meat is bad.

– Miller

The note is held to the fridge with the Oktoberfest magnet I purchased at Munich Airport before getting stuck in the toilet of my EasyJet flight and thinking I would die.

It is highly unusual for Miller to be thankful to the person who ruined his tub of ASDA-brand Neapolitan ice-cream. However, having just woken up, the subtleties of inter-household communication are currently beyond me.

I struggle to remember if it was me who left the freezer open the night before. Opening the tub, I see that the ice-cream has mutated into something postmodern. The pink stains the vanilla and what was once chocolate is now melted grey.

Reid, a housemate with questionable views on evolution, walks into the kitchen and proclaims that he feels gassy.

Reid asks me, 'Say, would you ever do a medical trial? It looks like good money.'

We both need the money as we are chronically unemployed.

I'm sleeping on a bed made of misshapen sofa cushions in the living room of a crowded London share house. Reid sleeps in a bed with a girlfriend whose phones calls he ignores, but stays with so that he doesn't have to sleep on the floor.

'Go on,' I say.

'Apparently we get to sit around eating free food, playing video games and getting paid over £1000 per week,' Reid says.

He sees Miller's note and laughs. He gets a spoon from the sink, rinses crusty oatmeal from the handle and starts eating the melted ice-cream straight from the tub.

'Let's just blame Cooky,' he says. Cooky forgets things. He smokes a lot and forgets things. Things like running the bath, then getting hungry and going to the supermarket, only to come back to discover he's stepped onto the set of *Waterworld*.

I remodel my bedroom back into a functioning living room and alternate between napping and bad TV. My phone beeps, interrupting the nothingness.

'Bong room, five minutes.'

The bong room has a particular aroma. Stale marijuana, household waste and wafts of what might be a decomposing hamster permeate the space. Our bong room is actually the bin room of the apartment complex. It is where we go to smoke cones in winter because it's too cold outside and Miller's girlfriend banned us from using the kitchen.

Cooky leans against a double-glazed window, a smile playing across his face. Ernie tells us they've just returned from Camden Market. They bought a bagful of magic mushrooms off a man with dreadlocks and then ate a curry from the food court.

COOKY EATS THE MUSHROOMS LIKE THEY ARE SALT AND VINEGAR POTATO CRISPS.

He barely swallows one fungi before two more are fisted down his gullet. 'Slow down,' Ernie says.

Cooky screws up his face like a child being told it isn't socially acceptable to put his hands down his underpants in public. He thinks we've been ripped off.

'The mushrooms aren't doing a thing,' Cooky insists.

'Why don't we head back into the living room. I'm keen to watch a doco on a family of militant Christians who think the world is going to end.'

Within 15 minutes, Ernie is staring at his hands like he's only just noticed them.

Cooky says, 'I think I made a bit of a mistake. The ceiling is moving. Not falling. Can anyone else see it? It's rolling in waves across the roof, like a plaster tide without a shore to break on.'

Cooky's girlfriend, Lakey, enters the room and says, 'We should go and get something to eat.' Ernie nods and grunts and sweats excessively.

We stumble into Real Burger, a burger chain that is slightly better than McDonald's but not as good as Hungry Jack's.

Cooky takes a seat and rests his head on the laminate table. He begins to hyperventilate into a brown paper bag that Ernie has swiped off the counter in a desperate attempt to calm him. Cooky sounds like a constipated donkey being strangled mid-bowel-movement.

People are looking. Lakey tells Cooky, 'Go to the bathroom and straighten yourself out.'

Cooky lumbers down a set of stairs in slow motion. He leans heavily on the handrail and apologises to people who aren't there for behaviour he has only imagined.

A boxed burger, the bun soggy from an excess of mayonnaise and old tomato, is slid onto the table in front of me. We eat our meals in silence.

Cooky has gone missing. After checking the male toilets, I confirm that he's not in the bathroom. Unsure of how long we've been sitting here, we begin to talk tactics for a search-and-rescue mission.

Suddenly, Cooky runs up the stairs saying we need to leave. Urgently. We dash outside. Streetlights illuminate the pavement. A light evening mist grows. We sprint down a pedestrian tunnel in tracksuit pants and winter jackets.

My stomach turns over chunks of barely chewed ground beef and two-day-old salad parts. We stop before I throw up.

Unsure why we just legged it three blocks, we shout at Cooky. 'Why the hell are we running? What happened? Why did we have to run away?' He eventually tells us he did make it to the Real Burger World bathrooms.

'So, I was standing in front of a basin, splashing water on my face for like 20 minutes. Trying to get myself sweet, but really unravelling in my own personal hell,' Cooky said.

'Finally, when I was trying to leave, a toilet cubicle door cracked open. Then some random old bird flipped it and screamed at me...'

'FUCKING

PERVERT!'

Disconnected from reality, Cooky had been barely keeping it together. He'd been throwing water around and talking to himself... in the middle of the female toilets.

TALES INTER-NATIO[NAL] PASTA

22

BELLAGIO, ITALY

OF AN

NAL

MULE

A thick, greasy film coats my skin. The torrential sweat doesn't dampen my shirt, it drowns it. With every shuffling movement of my feet I can feel their eyes on me.

They strut around with the puffed-out chests of a flightless bird looking for a mate. They wear navy-blue uniforms, stern expressions and appear to have undergone personality lobotomies during their induction. I know they are looking at me. Their eyes are drawn to my nervous appearance and enlarged stomach.

The security cameras appear to turn and follow my path as I walk down a short hallway. It's only a matter of time until I get stopped. It's only a matter of time until I appear on an episode of *Border Patrol*.

I fumble around in my pocket for my passport. It spills to the ground.

I have a waking nightmare involving rubber gloves, a dimly lit room and a customs officer smiling like a psychopath.

I wait an eternity for my luggage. I think about just leaving it at the airport and trying to rush through the final security checkpoint. Finally, my haggard suitcase is spat out onto the baggage carousel like a gristly piece of meat at a high-priced steak restaurant. I grab my luggage and wonder if they have already searched it. What have they found?

My ears drown in the noise of my thumping heart. It beats so fast, so loudly, that it echoes in my brain. I wheel my bag to the exit.

When I reach the front of the queue, a customs officer thrusts out a hand full of short, sausage-like fingers.

'Landing card and passport please,' he asks. His eyebrows rise when he takes in whatever coded note passport control had scribbled on it earlier.

I feel like gravity just got heavier. It's all too much. I can't take it anymore.

I blurt out, 'I'm not actually smuggling five kilos of heroin in my belly. I may look eight-months pregnant, but I've actually just eaten my body weight in food in Italy.'

Sausage Fingers frowns. He says, 'I didn't think you were an international drug mule, but, if you want, I can arrange for someone to check and just make sure.'

It's fair to say that I didn't pack on a modest layer of fat from eating in Italy, more that I evolved into a whale-like creature whose thick blubber could survive the coldest Antarctic waters. From fresh pastas oozing with creamy pesto-infused sauces, to risottos so thick they could cement brickwork in place, I ate everything Italy's Lombardy region could offer, and then went back for dessert.

The setting for my Italian feast was a small town called Bellagio that spilled down a lush green hillside to the edge of Lake Como. It was an elegant muddle of laneways overlooked by immaculately presented period houses, with overflowing flowerboxes on their narrow balconies.

Maria and I would normally rise early to gorge ourselves on sticky, sugar-powdered pastries at a waterfront café.

As the ferries docked at the small local port, we would watch as new waves of tourists from America, Germany and Russia descended upon the town like invading Vikings. Armed with credit cards and crisp euro notes, they would funnel into the town's laneways, ready to pillage the local tourist stores of their antiques, oil paintings and Italy-shaped fridge magnets. Against a backdrop of international accents trying to calculate exchange rates, we would sip at thick, dark, diesel-like coffees.

Since Roman times, Lake Como has been a popular retreat for the wealthy residents of nearby Milan. The lake is the third-largest in Italy and is watched over by both an army of paparazzi looking for a drunken celebrity to snap, and a jagged mountain range that cuts angular silhouettes at sunset.

The roads linking the towns of Lake Como are not easy driving. The asphalt streets twist and turn and hug the shores of the deep blue lake. During peak tourist season, the traffic is so bad that it stands still. The Lake Como ferry system is a far better way to move around. The ferries have unobstructed views of postcard-perfect, stone-built towns and you are washed over by a cooling breeze standing on the outside deck. Many lazy hours were spent criss-crossing the lake on our holiday.

One afternoon, we shuffled onto the ferry going to the village of Varenna to graze like two fattened cows being readied for slaughter.

A shady promenade follows the Varennese shoreline. We walked past elegant villas and cobblestone alleyways with steps and archways leading up to the main piazza. Inevitably though, our stomachs drew us, like Shane Warne to a peroxide convention, to one of Varenna's small lakeside restaurants.

The menu unfolds across four massive pages. Vines suffocate a stunted tree and run along thin wires, forming a deep green canopy above the sitting diners.

Our waiter looks like Salvador Dalí. His moustache is waxed into long spears. The greasy lengths of facial hair jut out above his mouth. He waves his hands expansively as he describes his favourite dishes on the menu.

'I'm not here to fuck spiders,' I say, knowing it won't translate. 'Let's just try one of each of the house specialities and see how we go.'

I point to a range of the specialties on the menu. Maria clears her throat. She rests her hand on my protruding belly and raises a single eyebrow.

Dalí Moustache smiles. Speaking in a thick Italian accent, he tells us, 'Not to worry.' He moves his hands like he is drawing in the air and simply says, 'L'appetito vien mangiando' or,

'APPETITE COMES WITH EATING.'

THE M
OF BR
RELATIO

23

ZAGREB, CROATIA

USEUM
OKEN
NSHIPS

A noxious haze blurs the horizon. Roads choke on an unmoving flow of cars that spew out diesel and Eastern European pop music. Clusters of plaster-clad concrete apartment towers look down across the city.

The late summer air is static, heavy and humid. The streetscape has an ethereal glow. Lampposts sway in the distance like an urban mirage. The shade under the plane tree in Zrinjevac Park gives no respite to parched tourists. Sun-scorched leaves die on the branch, tree roots ache with thirst.

I wipe dirt from my Ray-Bans onto a white t-shirt. Streaks of grime colour the lower hem.

I hear the coffee shop before I see it. Words and the smell of tobacco float across bands of friends and casual acquaintances. The bitter vapour from a hand-rolled cigarette falls out of a university student's mouth. Taxi drivers, students and office workers crowd the pavement on green plastic chairs.

A skinny waiter with a greasy ponytail is working for tips and moves at the sound of a customer clearing his throat.

She messages me a photo from last night. The picture is of the back of my head at a bar before she introduced herself, drank my vodka cranberry and asked, 'Did you choose that drink because you're in touch with your feminine side, or do you just have a UTI?'

I told her that I found American accents annoying. She said good thing that she was from Vancouver then.

Ponytail glides across paved stone without effort, moving like he is one of the undead. Sweat stains his white linen shirt. I stumble through some phrase-book Croatian and order a coffee and a short glass of rakia.

I message the girl from Vancouver, 'Wow, thanks. Way to capture my best angle. What are you up to? What are we doing today?'

A student with thin-rimmed glasses and inconsistent facial hair leans over. He asks, in broken English, 'Can you light my cigarette please?'

Ponytail materialises out of nowhere, handing the student a box of matches. He drops two glasses on the table and pours the rakia from a great height. I am about to mention that I only ordered one shot, when he picks up the other glass and drinks it himself.

Vancouver sends me a photo of an empty tub of yoghurt. She asks, 'Do you I like to cry? Do you feel like bathing in other people's grief and self-pity? I'm going to the Museum of Broken Relationships. It should be a hilarious, depressing mess and I don't want to go alone. Come with me?'

Later, I am stranded on a street corner, waiting for her to arrive. I feel awkward, exposed. I suddenly become self-aware of my hands. What should I be doing with them?

Someone taps me on my left shoulder. When I turn around, there is no one there. I turn back and there and suddenly Vancouver is standing there in front of me, laughing.

'What the fuck are you doing with your fingers? Why are you being so odd?' she asks.

The Museum of Broken Relationships is a cultural punch in the face. It is a museum dedicated to failed love, taking submissions from break-ups around the world.

A vinyl record hangs from a white wall, a simple note reads that 'A submission from a teenage break-up 30 years ago.' It is clear that the record owner still isn't over it.

Vancouver says, 'Oh I'd love to listen to that record. Take a swim in the owner's pain.'

'I get the distinct impression that you were a goth in high school,' I say.

She smiles a crooked smile, says, 'Oh no. I was far too uncool for that.'

A malnourished collection of urban-foraging hipsters from Berlin carrying canvas tote bags bearing Angela Merkel's face enter the space

They crowd around a black suspender belt displayed in a glass case like it is the *Mona Lisa*. The suspender belt hangs in isolation. The owner's caption reads, 'I never wore them. The relationship might have lasted longer if I had.'

The girl from Vancouver holds my hand. She doesn't talk, but when she stands in front of a display that means something to her, she squeezes my palm a little tighter.

She laughs aloud at a display featuring a candy G-string captioned with, 'After four years, he turned out to be as cheap and unthoughtful as his presents.'

A small wooden table holds a book filled with empty white pages. A pen sits in the folds of paper. An exhibit note invites visitors to write about their own broken relationships.

Vancouver asks me, 'So how do you think we'll end?'

I look away and say, 'I'm not sure.' I'm getting on a plane to Switzerland in two days.

The museum exits through a reasonably priced gift shop. I tell the girl from Vancouver that a session with a counsellor, rather than break-up kitsch, would probably sell better than the fridge magnets on display.

The outside world is harsh, bathing in a post-apocalyptic heat. The sun's rays scorch on impact and my mouth dries on drawing breath.

Vancouver shields her eyes when looking at me. I would offer her my sunglasses, but don't know what the gesture would suggest.

Vancouver says, 'I've got to leave. But I bought you something that will help.' She kisses me with salty, dry lips and tells me, 'In public, stop looking at your hands like they are someone else's.'

Vancouver pushes a small, brown paper bag into my palm and walks away. I feel like a bad actor in an even worse movie.

I want her to turn around. I want to run after her and ask if she has any plans for dinner. Instead, I slump into the shade of a bus shelter.

I open the brown paper bag and pull out a novelty pencil rubber from the gift shop. On it are the words:

I would never see her again.

STREET FIGHTING IN IBIZA

24 IBIZA, SPAIN

1:00 AM

A hand is on my neck. My arm is crudely twisted behind my back. I've been picked up and rushed down a set of nondescript stairs. Someone shouts my name. Not in a 'Great to see you again, we should catch up soon,' kind of way. More of a 'Fuck. Do I call your mum if your body doesn't turn up in two days?' vibe.

My head is slammed painfully against the door. Once. Twice. Three times. The door opens, and I am airborne. Floating in slow motion like a flightless bird in a cartoon walking off a cliff, my limbs flail. I brace for impact. I've been hurled out of one biggest nightclub's in Ibiza into an empty carpark.

I land hard. Roll three times.

I'm flat on my back. I have bitumen on my t-shirt, gravel embedded into my skin. In the background, I hear the crowd erupt as Maxi from Faithless takes to the stage. All I can think is that my friends are still in there. I have to get back in.

Picking myself up, I run around the outside of the nightclub towards the front door. I convince myself that taking my t-shirt off and turning it inside out will be enough to make me unrecognisable.

Hiding my bloodied elbow behind my back, I sidestep the line at the front door to Privilege Ibiza. Walking to the front of the queue, I nonchalantly say 'I lost my wristband pass-out. Can I come back in?'

The girl at the club door looks at me suspiciously. She says the Spanish equivalent for 'Bugger off or buy a ticket and line up again.' I complain and hold up the line behind me for so long that eventually she just waves me through.

She shoots me a look that says, 'You're clearly a bit of a fuckhead.' She would see plenty like me that night.

Like a conquering Roman emperor, I emerge out of the sweaty dance floor and swagger towards my friends. My arms are raised in triumph. Expectant that my return would be told to future generations with wonder and amazement.

But they didn't even realise I'd been gone.

'Shit. Didn't you see me get picked up by that gorilla of a security guard?' I yelled at them. 'He threw me out of the nightclub for climbing on the roof looking for a toilet.'

My friends nodded but clearly didn't hear me. Or understand.

One observed, 'Hey, why is your t-shirt on inside out?' Like I'd made a mistake when getting ready for the night and he was the first to notice.

Another asked, 'Did you get me anything from the bar?' As if that were where I'd been for the last half hour.

4:00 AM

The ocean laps lazily under a crescent moon. Morning is not far away. A couple involved in some heavy petting on a sun lounge are interrupted by a security guard.

A hotel worker pours chlorine into a kidney bean-shaped swimming pool that bathers had an 80 per cent chance of catching herpes in.

I watch it all from our apartment balcony, nursing a warm beer. Out of nowhere, there is a knock on our apartment door. I look at Matty as a rumbling noise reverberates down the hallway like rolling thunder.

In walks in a mountain of a man with a thick Eastern European accent. With huge, muscular arms covered in tattoos, he looked like Zangief from Street Fighter II. He walks into the kitchen and helps himself to a beer.

Pete asked Zangief, 'You lost, mate?' Maybe he mistook our apartment for his own. An easy mistake Pete himself could understand.

5:00 PM

(the day before)

With a belly full of beer and mild heat stroke, Pete wobbled back from the beach. He needed a lie down. Or at least a glass of water. Pete clumsily fondled his pockets looking for a key that wasn't there. Luckily, the apartment door was open.

Pete walked in. He was surprised to find a couple of friendly Spanish guys with their feet up in the living room. They waved warmly. Pete assumed they were friends of ours. Being a generous host, Pete went to the fridge and gave the Spanish guys a beer. They looked at him curiously but drank and started a conversation.

More Spanish people arrived with another case of beer. 'No worries fellas. Make yourselves at home,' Pete said.

Beers were opened and discussions in broken English were endured.

All was going well, until Pete saw some of the Spanish guys start going into the bedrooms.

'Hey! Get out of there. Stay out of our rooms and get your hands off our things!' he called. 'You can have a beer in the living room – but stay out of the bedrooms.'

The Spanish guys looked confused. They laughed. Then went back into the bedrooms. Pete wasn't having this.

'Get the fuck out of our bedrooms,' he yelled.

He pushed one of the Spanish guys. Told them all it was time to leave. The Spanish guys got angry. They corrected Pete. Told him he was their guest, but now it was time to go. They pushed Pete put of the apartment and slammed the door after him.

Pete was about to kick at the door when he saw the apartment number. 109 not 108. He was supposed to be next door.

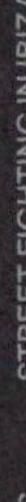

4:30 AM

Zangief settles in on the living room sofa. He takes his shirt off and throws it across the room. He slams three beers down and starts calling us 'My friends!'

But something is not right. His stories are erratic, and he is giving off a distinct, 'I have several bodies buried in hand-dug shallow graves around the island' vibe.

'Look mate, we're going to call it a night. We're just really tired so it's probably best if you leave,' Matty says to Zangief.

He isn't listening. He starts telling a story that no one can follow. We cut Zangief off. No more beers.

Zangief grows agitated, 'I thought we were friends!?'

I say, 'We don't even know you, or why you are in our room.' His face changes.

Zangief now looks angry. He stands up and starts swearing.

'Jebi se!' he spits at us.

Everyone in the room now insists that Zangief leave. Zangief throws a beer can across the room. Yells some more. Eventually though, he walks away, stumbling down the hallway. He slams a door loudly. Calls us 'Sons of whores!'

No sooner have we locked the door than something slams against it. The door rattles on its hinges. Zangief is yelling outside the apartment.

'You dirty thieves. You stole my shirt!'

He wants the same crumpled, sweat-stained, paper-thin item of clothing that he had taken off and thrown across the room.

Matty goes over and picks up the t-shirt. He is furious with Zangief for ruining our night. He walks down the hall towards the front door with the t-shirt, pausing to shove it down his pants and use it to wipe his arse in an unnecessarily aggressive manner.

Propping the door open, Matty throws the t-shirt out to Zangief and tells him to 'Fuck off!' before slamming and locking the apartment door.

We laugh. Beers are opened. Discussion turns to the worst way to die at the hands of a Street Fighter II character.

Zangief is back and kicking at the door. He is screaming

'YOU DICKS. DON'T CHEAT ME! THIS IS NOT MY SHIRT.'

The t-shirt Matty had thrown to him was not his own. Zangief was right: his t-shirt is still sitting in the corner of the room.

Everyone stops talking. We look around the room nervously. If that wasn't Zangief's t-shirt, then what did Matty just wipe his arse with?

After a careful negotiation, Matty enters the hallway and exchanges t-shirts through Zangief's half-opened doorway.

Watching from the living room, I see Matty stop halfway back down the hallway, like he has lost his way. His torso crumples in defeat. The room is still. Silent.

'Fuck,' says Matty.

The bum-stained t-shirt was his own.

25

DON'T BE A WANKER

BINTAN ISLAND, INDONESIA

Small, turquoise waves break close to shore. Sun-kissed bodies sprawl across plastic lounges and beach towels as palm trees sway to a rhythmic breeze. The scorching hot sand is a fine, white powder that squeaks and burns my feet with every step I take.

It feels like I'm walking through the set of a 1980s tourism commercial, with the addition of a handful of bloated English tourists wearing replica Chelsea football jerseys and paying for local women to drink with them and laugh at their jokes. Northern Indonesia has more postcard-perfect beaches than a Bondi-based coke dealer has mobile phones. I can't help but want more.

Beach holidays are usually an unwanted item on my travel itinerary. To me, fly-and-flop tropical holidays are about as welcome as a fresh cold sore making an appearance ahead of a date with a long-term crush. 'No, it's not facial herpes. Although it does come from the same viral family...'

Thankfully, while the island of Bintan is a haven for sun-seeking layabouts a short ferry ride from Singapore, there is more to the destination than just shaking the sand out of your bum crack at the end of the day.

I had recently almost crippled myself riding quad bike over uneven terrain, snorkelled with a plastic bag I mistook for a deadly jellyfish and ate a lovely meal that was either soft-shell crab or heavily marinated spider – I still do not know.

The receptionist at the resort where I've been staying wears a sinister, permanent sneer that leads me to assume the wind changed while he was strangling a kitten.

Kitten Strangler tells me, 'Your car is arriving soon. You have some time before the ferry leaves, so you could stop for a meal on the way.'

Kitten Strangler gestures for me to follow him to the check-out desk. I walk behind him through a cloud of cheap aftershave. He begins to alternate between English and Bahasa, which I don't understand. From what I pick up from Kitten Strangler, I'll either be sharing the car with an elderly couple from Canada or lunch service finishes at 2pm.

A black, polished Toyota arrives shortly after and a portly taxi driver greets me with a toothy grin.

'So where do you want to go boss?' Toothy Grin asks as we pull away from the resort.

'If we have time before the ferry leaves, I'd love to see Panglong Village,' I reply.

'Okay. Okay. We can do.'

Our taxi turns off a coastal road and cuts through the heart of the island. We drive east on a road flanked by thick jungle.

Shadows play across the path in front of us.

'Are you sure you don't want to play some golf?' asks Toothy Grin. 'I know a course that has very pretty girls. Very pretty caddies. When you hit the ball off the course into the jungle, they will follow you in to help find it.

'You will have a very good time looking for your ball with these girls. Trust me,' Toothy Grin laughs, making an obscene gesture with his hand.

'Nah, I'm good thanks mate. Golf just isn't my thing,' I say, looking down at my phone but trying not to be rude.

The taxi slows. A child runs across the road, clutching a rubber ball in his arms. His father protests and gives chase. The sun breaks through a bank of clouds and illuminates tinned rooftops as Panglong Village comes into view.

Known as the village of the Sea People, or 'Orang Suku Laut', Panglong is home to Bintan's historic nomadic fishing community. The village was developed with the government to provide the families a more stable existence, rather than always living at sea, permanently moving.

Inside the village, a deeply tanned local crouches over a fishing net, pulling at a hole he has just fixed, testing its strength. I slowly follow a walkway overhanging the water. I look out over houses that stand atop wooden stilts, looking like one strong wind would blow them away.

A skinny wooden boat makes its way out to sea, the men inside it waving to those in another small vessel coming in to shore. There is a calming, rhythmic feel to the village, like every day is much the same. The strong smell of dried fish is everywhere, yet no one (besides me) seems to notice, or even care.

Toothy Grin is suddenly behind me, saying that we must go, 'No. No. No. I thought you were on the later ferry. We have a long way back: we need to leave now,' he urges. 'Hurry, hurry. We don't want to be late!'

Rain hits worn bitumen. Dust turns to mud. Our Toyota cuts rapidly through the heavy tropical air. A lonely traffic light at a deserted intersection shows red, but we drive on, trying to make up time. The Bintan landscape is a blur, one patch of green foliage by the roadside unrecognisable from the next.

At the ferry terminal, I try and remain calm at the slow pace of the people moving along the dock. The sun is out in force, causing me to perspire heavily. I suddenly become aware that my back sweat's migratory path has come to its unpleasant, but unsurprising, final resting place in my underpants.

The ferry pushes away from Bintan Island. As the boat drifts away from the tree-covered landmass, I feel my mobile phone vibrate in my pocket.

Before I can answer it, we move out of range of reception. I move to the back of the boat and to recapture a signal. I try holding my arm in the air, but nothing works.

I approach a small on-board kiosk to ask for the Wi-Fi password. An old lady sits behind a wooden counter selling bottles of cold Pepsi and dried fruit in small plastic bags. She doesn't answer me, just waves her hand to indicate I should move out of the way and stop blocking her paying customers.

I walk away from the kiosk in frustration. The lack of Wi-Fi shouldn't bother me. But it does.

Our boat moves across a lumpy blanket of slow-moving water. Small, rocky outcrops cast elegant shadows in the late of the day.

I slump into a cracked leather seat as the boat rolls peacefully over a coming wave. I realise at this exact moment, in the middle of what could be close to some kind of tropical paradise, that...

I MAY, (UNFORTUNATELY) BE AN ACTUAL, FIRST-WORLD WANKER.

But maybe I always was.

BROKEN BY THE CITY

26

NEW YORK CITY, USA

CASA BELLA
RISTORANTE
BAR
NAPOLI
NAPOLI
FAMOUS GIFTS

There is blood on my left shoe. A man wearing a tweed jacket looks twice at me before getting into the elevator. His pungent vanilla cologne makes me gag.

They say every city is different. Some are best visited for their artistic wonders, some for unique architecture and others just to eat your way through their market-laden streets. But not this city.

This city simply exists to kick your arse. This city leaves your bank account as scarcely populated as a beach after an appearance by Tony Abbott in a pair of tight Speedos. This city will leave your once-healthy body on the verge of near-permanent decay. This city will laugh in your face as you crawl, defeated, on all fours back to the airport, desperately seeking a flight home.

And if this city hasn't left you regretting your life choices, without contemplating a lengthy stint in a rehab facility, well, you just haven't done it properly.

New York City is high functioning. It performs at its peak all of the time. Like an insomniac who has just smoked a couple of kilos of crystal meth, sleep just isn't an option for the island of Manhattan. The city assaults your ears with the maddening urban symphony of people with somewhere to go and a very limited time to get there.

The elevator door jolts open and I drink in greedy waves of the stale, artificially cooled air. I blink against the harsh yellow light of the hotel lobby and shuffle across the waxed marble floor. The concierge appears in front of me like the unwanted arrival of a recurring venereal disease.

'I watch you coming into the hotel every morning,' the concierge says, and starts to rapid-fire questions at me. 'How are you enjoying your stay? What have you seen? Have you been over to Brooklyn yet?'

My voice breaks. It's like puberty never happened, as I struggle to push a sentence between my teeth. I give up and smile apologetically. The truth is that I can't answer the question. I can't reel off a list of landmarks, museums or five-starred eateries at which I have indulged.

From the moment I landed at JFK Airport, my personal finances have been put on a starvation diet as I swelled my liver through the dive bars of East Village, the nightclubs of the Meatpacking District and the alcohol-soaked after-hours drinking dens of Manhattan.

The skin on my face is grey. It hangs loosely. The only sunlight I have seen are the morning's first rays between soaring concrete and glass towers from the back seat of a yellow cab heading home.

I step out onto 13th Street, swaying unsteadily. It feels like the whole world wants to push past me. An elderly lady, with a dead fox around her shoulder, stubs my toe with a walking cane and snarls at me.

I put on a pair of sunglasses and turn away from the madness of Times Square. I shuffle uptown towards Central Park. Rich, poor, athletically preppy or morbidly gothic, Central Park welcomes everyone.

From the moneyed Wall Street joggers desperate to keep their heart rates high, to the Fifth Avenue nannies dragging on nicotine sticks on their breaks, Central Park is a cross-section of the city in between doing other things. New York in its spare time.

I collapse onto a dark green park bench and overlook a group of street performers re-enacting scenes from Shakespeare to a sweltering tourist-heavy audience. A violinist walks through the park, shaking a metal tin looking for tips.

One of my friends proposed to his girlfriend in Central Park yesterday. He hired mountain bikes at sunset and they rode around the park with a bottle of wine in his backpack and a placeholder engagement ring weighing heavy in his pocket.

He kept pulling off the road into secluded parts of the park, looking for a private clearing where he could ask the big question. She kept asking him why he was slowing down. It would be dark soon and if they didn't hurry up they would probably have their skins shaved off with blunt razors by a man who would wear their faces at dinner parties held with other socially ambitious Manhattan-based psychopaths.

Eventually, he found what he thought was the perfect spot. They relaxed on the grass. He appeared nervous, she asked what was wrong. He let out a grunt and got down on a knee. She said yes.

It was a genuinely romantic story, except for the fact he was kneeling on broken glass and there was a homeless guy playing with his junk 10 metres away.

The sun sinks slowly between the silhouettes of grey towers that overlook Central Park West. Long shadows are cast over a softball field where nobody really seems to be keeping score.

My watch tells me I am late. I hail a taxi from 59th Street. The inside of the taxi smells like an Italian restaurant delivery van. I give the driver an address in Hell's Kitchen.

The restaurant is a heaving with people jostling for tables, waiters juggling plates of food and fashionably malnourished people trying to look achingly cool in a small space without adequate air conditioning.

Waiting at a bar for a friend, I sit next to a couple from Seattle. Their skin looks clear and healthy, like they were born fresh at age 26.

The man from Seattle says, 'This is our first night in the city. We haven't been on vacation in over a year, so we're pretty excited.'

'Why didn't you pick somewhere more relaxing for your vacation?

Somewhere with a beach?' I ask.

'Oh, we thought about it. But we wanted to come to New York to feed off its energy, like a shot of adrenaline,' Seattle says.

I COUGH AND IT SOUNDS LIKE MY INTERNAL ORGANS ARE TRYING TO ESCAPE THROUGH MY MOUTH

I list some bars and restaurants that they might like to visit. Out of nowhere, I blurt out, 'I'm leaving the city soon.'

Seattle puts a sympathetic arm on my shoulder. 'I had an aunt who lived in New York for 15 years – but one day it just became too much. For her health, for her sanity, she had to pack up and leave.'

Seattle says that sometimes, you can have too much of a good thing.

'How long have you lived in the city for anyway?' Seattle asks.

I laugh and it hurts more than it really should. I tell him, '... less than a week.'

DON'T EAT THE

27

CAIRO, EGYPT

ALAWEYAT

I was about to explode. Again.

My head pulsated like an over-abused strobe light at a bad rave. I was choking on vomit, sweat coated my body and my bowels were acting like I'd swallowed a grenade. I wished I could step outside my body.

Maria and I hailed down a Cairo death cab. With four bald tires, no seatbelts, a patchwork frame and the strong smell of dirty petrol, the vehicle would have sooner qualified as a multi-person coffin than as an actual motorcar. I pointed to the address of the historical Mena House hotel and sat back as our toothless taxi driver rocketed into the night.

Maria squeezed my hand as I let out a groan. There was no one else to blame but me.

It was night three of our holiday. The past few days had been a pre-planned package-holiday tourist dream. We stayed in five-star luxury, lazed by a swimming pool, woke up every morning to a direct view of the pyramids. The only problem was that it didn't seem real.

From the moment we were greeted at the airport by our Arab tour guide, with an English accent, we had been wrapped in an air-conditioned bubble. English Accent directed our driver, dealt with entrance guards at museums and the pyramids, shepherded away persistent street merchants and even negotiated which view of the pyramids our room should have with the hotel front desk.

All that changed when I told English Accent to take the day off. We're up for a little exploring of our own. Little did I realise that walking the streets of Cairo would soon become an experiment in how much dust you could inhale without dying.

When the sun sat high in the sky and my stomach began to rumble, I suggested to Maria that it was time for lunch. Street-food style.

Street food was big in Cairo long before it became the eating style du jour among hipsterrific, ironic beard cultivators. But the local street-food providers in Egypt's capital don't lower themselves to menus polluted with hybrid-fusion-Vietnamese with South American super grains to cater for evangelistic, Paleo-exclusive, CrossFit narcissists. Rather, they focus on delivering unapologetically calorie-laden food at good prices, right at street level.

Moreish falafel, freshly baked Arabic breads, delicious minced marinated lamb kofta kebabs: the streets of Cairo are a roll call of culinary classic hits.

Given I was looking to immerse myself in the local ways, I decided it was time to...

EAT AS THE LOCALS DO.

I approached a street-food stall selling halaweyat. Basically, this is a pot full of random – and better left unanalysed – lamb parts boiling in their own grease. The halaweyat was dished up to me with a chunk of Arabic bread.

English Accent texted me as the day slipped into night. He wrote, 'What are you guys doing tonight? Come out and have a drink and see a different part of Egypt, if you have no plans.'

Still feeling fine, I graciously accepted his offer, keen to experience the real Cairo after dark.

The French Club was a popular open-air bar for consulate workers and select friends. We met our guide at the front door, where we were asked to sign in.

As we were putting pen to paper, the manager approached our group. 'You,' he said, pointing at English Accent. 'You cannot come in!'

'Why?' I asked. 'Because he's Egyptian,' the manager answered.

English Accent looked angry. He looked embarrassed. He talked with an East London accent and knew more words in the English language than I did. Yet he was in his own country and was being told that he cannot enter a building by a fellow Egyptian, because he's Egyptian. I didn't know what to say.

Maria and I made a stand and began to argue. To avoid a scene, we were eventually ushered in through a side door. At the bar, English Accent told us that this situation shouldn't cloud our thinking of his country. There were a lot of things wrong with the old ways, he said, but one day that would change.

We settled in at a table under a handful of stars as a jazz band began to play. Two wooden sticks danced lightly across the skin of the snare drum. The trumpeter's cheeks ballooned out, looking like his face could burst if prodded by a strategically placed pin. Fingers plucked at the double bass and the pianist was lost in a solo, forgetting there was anyone around. The beer was cold and our guide's friends were welcoming.

A mishmash collection of locals and expats sat around under an open sky laughing at the insanity of the city. Shaking their heads at what it had become.

عطفة الحمام
entranc

I went completely white. Maria asked me if I was feeling okay. I tried to dismiss the audible rumblings of my stomach as the noise from an aircraft flying low overhead.

AROUND THIS TIME I BEGAN TO REGRET THE HALAWEYAT.

Halfway through our sixth beer (and after committing several crimes against humanity in the bathroom), I admitted defeat. With a few quick goodbyes, I ran out of the bar, with Maria giving chase.

On the freeway home, our taxi driver attempted to break the land speed record. It was a terrifying experience. The back windows of the car did not even wind up. We are blasted with a constant flow of air, heavy with pollution.

Maria closed her eyes out of fear. I bent over double from pain. The taxi made close calls with an overladen fruit truck and a commuter bus. I sat upright with a thumping chest and wondered if we would ever see the air-conditioned wonder of our hotel room again.

I wanted to see the real Egypt. Our toothless driver laughed as it hurtled past me at over 160km/h.

28

COLORADO, USA

THE COOKIES WERE A BAD IDEA

Gravel fractures under the weight of rubber-soled feet. The path winds upwards. It hugs the side of a cliff face. Like skin, it wears the mountain's undulations.

The valley floor spills out beneath us. Streams of melted snow merge into a shimmering emerald river that runs through the basin gorge. Children play in the shallows of the river beside parents who stand ankle-deep, assessing the current and responding to work emails marked 'high importance' on their mobile phones.

I pause on the outside edge of the walking trail to let a group of health-conscious, cargo-shorted seniors pass. One of their group exhibits a mobile-phone holder on his leather belt. They all nod and say hello. I steal a look over the path's edge. A heaped pile of broken boulders at the base of the mountain hints that things are not as permanent as they first seemed.

'Hold up... Slow down... Can we take a breather?' Chris pants.

The previously separate sweat stains underneath his man boobs join to make a smiley face on his t-shirt. Chris gulps down huge mouthfuls of air.

'FUCK ME THAT AIR IS CLEAN… EACH BREATH IS LIKE

INHALING

AN ANGEL'S FART'

A hang-glider tries to outrun its shadow. It twists, turns and dives attempting to outsmart the sun above. We track the glider with our eyes as it crosses the valley, an effortless nomad in the air.

'I think we made a mistake. Those hash cookies were a bad idea,' James says. 'My feet are so heavy. It feels like they're being weighed down.'

We turn, take the path downwards in silence. At the base of the hiking trail, the healthy seniors sit eating homemade salads from Tupperware. They clean their boots in the river before driving away in their Toyota SUV.

'The Rocky Mountains are bullshit. I just want to lie down on a couch and watch TV,' Chris whines.

On the outskirts of Telluride village, we pass the grounds of a music festival. Canvas tents populate the roadside, dirty clothes hang on thin ropes and tree branches. Over a loudspeaker, Ryan Adams sings about heartache to a lonely banjo, as middle-aged men huddle and discuss their favourite craft beer.

We wait for a gondola to take us up and out of the valley.

Behind us is a family eating ice-creams. A little boy drops his and begins to cry.

'I'd have a sook as well, little man,' Chris sympathises. 'The thing looked bloody delicious.'

The ground quickly falls away from beneath us. Hanging by a metal wire, our gondola drifts up the face of the mountain as if powered by an unseen tide. We skim the tops of pine trees and bear trails. The village grows smaller below. The main street is a carpark of pick-up trucks and people carrying American flags that wave limply in a weak breeze.

At the top of the mountain, we exit the moving gondola and take a large, cream van with tan leather seats and a powerful air conditioner back to our house.

The kitchen is a crime scene of midnight snacking. Open packets of tortilla chips spill across a stone bench, chocolate Oreos stand erect in a tub of garlic hummus. Chris channel-surfs from the vantage of a soft, brown sofa as James, standing at the fridge, asks who wants a beer.

My eyes close to the low hum of background conversation, something about making connecting flights out of Denver later in the week. A pillow hits my face with a softened violence.

I swear.

'Shut up,' Chris snaps. 'You should be watching this!'

A documentary on life in Siberia plays out plays out on the TV screen. Images of thick, foreboding forests, bulging hills and frost-covered villages draw our attention.

Chris sighs, 'The world really is an amazing place.'

We bathe in the artificial light of a TV screen as outside a swollen, tired sun falls beneath the horizon. The summit of a towering, snow-capped mountain illuminates for an instant against the fading light: a pure white peak painted onto a rapidly darkening canvas.

THE P

G PEN

She looks horrified. The deep, Southern European tan drains from her face. It was as if she had found me crouching behind a door holding a bloodied meat cleaver and a dating guide written by Charles Manson.

She shrieks, 'You're not wearing any underwear... Are you?'

Her words created sickening revolutions in my stomach, like the time I drank the liquid from a jar of pickled cucumbers on a drunken dare in a hostel kitchen in Prague.

I cough up a mouthful of tepid beer. I don't have a clue how to answer her. We have only just met. We are in a giant Bavarian beer hall surrounded by thousands of people and I don't even know her name.

My mind does a quick catalogue check of the rancid pairs of boxer shorts that I still have in rotation after backpacking for six months. I was pushing the limits of what one would consider acceptable levels of personal hygiene. I shudder. Panic.

'Why yes, I am,' I try to answer in my deepest voice, before adding, 'but I can very easily lose them if the occasion calls for it?'

Her face screws up, folding in on itself to create deep creases across her face as if she'd just tasted rotten meat.

'What?' she asks, starting to laugh.

'Ewww. No! Don't be stupid. I was just asking for your own safety.'

She raises a twisted, bony finger in the air and points at the inflatable pig hovering with menace above.

The pig has a manic expression painted on its rubbery features. It hangs precariously by thin metal wires over a sweaty, drunken, heaving mass of bodies.

The pig is naked but for a collection of small pieces of cloth of various colours draped over its ears and back. As I stare at the pig, she leans towards my ear and yells, 'You still don't get it do you?'

'Well, no not really. I mean a piece of leopard-print cloth on the pig's ear, next to some bright blue cloth... It just doesn't work for me,' I reply.

'No, you idiot,' she says. 'It's not whether the cloth on the pig matches or not, it's what the cloth is.'

No sooner had the fresh spittle that accompanies her words infested my ear than I got to witness, with rising fear, what she meant.

A group of muscular South African men start cheering as they hoist a dreadlocked backpacker up above their shoulders – by his boxer shorts. They pull him off the ground, as his shorts disappear up his rear end.

Suddenly, the dreadlocked backpacker falls to the ground and one of the South African men hoists a pair of tattered boxer shorts over his head in primal triumph. He roars, and the trophy underwear is hoisted high in the air, before being thrown at the big, pink pig.

I turn and push against a tide of thrashing limbs, making my way to the exit as quickly as I can. I burst out of the beer hall and start running. There is no one following me, but that doesn't stop my legs from pushing against the ground with all their might.

I fall over breathless and exhausted some 20 metres from the beer hall. A German family gives me odd looks as I shove my hands down the front of my pants to check I'm still wearing underwear.

People tell you many things about Oktoberfest before you arrive. They tell you about the seven million litres of beer served and how you'll be drinking with six million other people from all around the world.

What they don't tell you, though, is that if you enter the 'Pig Pen' in the Hofbräuhaus beer hall wearing underwear, you do so at your own risk.

My mobile phone flashes a message from Cale. He has been missing all day. He asks where I am and says he had a problem. A peculiar one.

We meet outside a sausage truck. I am about to regale him with my tale of escape from the South African boxer-short police, when he launches into his own tale of woe.

'Hey, you remember those roast chickens we ate last night?' he starts.

'Kind of... Why?' My memories of our first night at Oktoberfest are hazy at best. Cale says

PAULANER

'YOU DIDN'T HAPPEN TO EAT ANY OF THE BONES, DID YOU?'

'I was fairly inebriated last night, but no,' I say. 'I'm pretty sure I didn't eat any chicken bones last night, Cale, because last time I checked I wasn't a dog, or a caveman.'

'Ahh, okay. Cool. Just asking ... ' he sheepishly trails off.

'Why? Did you Cale?'

'Maybe. Not sure really. Could have, I guess. I've been crapping out bits of chicken bone this morning so maybe I did. It really hurts. I have blood coming out of my bum. Maybe I need help,' Cale says timidly.

We go in search of a first-aid tent and a quiet place to have a beer. Settling in at the Paulaner beer hall, I'm serenaded by traditional German folk music, beer orders being shouted at full voice and Cale grunting as he tries to sit down.

'Don't even think about laughing. No one can understand the pain I'm going through right now,' Cale warns me.

'Oh, I wouldn't be so sure,' I reply. 'There's a dreadlocked backpacker limping around Munich right now who can probably relate.'

MARCH OF THE MUD PEOPLE

30

THE DEAD SEA, JORDAN

A shadow skims the pale desert sand. A lonely bird labours across the sky, lost and out of place. The sun is angry. Unforgiving. Its full, hostile force means that the interior of the car goes from air-conditioned comfort to something resembling a sauna endurance contest as soon as a window is opened.

Coming over the mountain pass, a vast turquoise lagoon spills out across the valley.

The scene is otherworldly. Sun-scorched barren hilltops frame an environment that looks more like the backdrop to a 1970s sci-fi movie than one of Jordan's best-known tourist attractions, the Dead Sea.

The road we are on winds and twists a path down to the basin floor. Our driver seems intent on testing our claims that no one present is prone to car sickness. He laughs and sings off-key to Arabic pop music. He brakes late into corners (and sometimes not at all).

We arrive near the water's edge and the smell is of another place. Stepping out of the vehicle my nostrils fill with the scent of the seashore. Wafts of briny, salty air brings back memories of beachside family vacations. I half expect to hear my mother yelling in the distance for me to put on another layer of sunscreen before I go swimming. The smell is of the beach, but we are nowhere near an ocean.

The lowest point on the surface of Earth, the Dead Sea sits some 430 metres below sea level. It is, in fact, not a sea at all. It is a lake, and a rather salty one at that. As the main tributary of the Jordan River, the Dead Sea is where the river ends, its evaporating waters leaving behind vast beds of salt and minerals.

Someone grips my arm. Their nails dig into my flesh. I am about to protest with a flurry of profanities when I see it. Or rather, I see *them*.

They stagger limb-locked at the water's edge, moving slowly, awkwardly. Their dark brown skin is hard and scaly like they have just emerged, freshly baked, from a giant oven.

'The migration of the Mud People,' a friend says, channelling his best David Attenborough voice, and no one disagrees.

Mud-covered tourists are a common fixture along the banks of the Dead Sea. People scoop mud from clay buckets, spreading it liberally across their skin like they are icing a child's birthday cake. They sit and cook the mud into their skin under the giant sunlamp in the sky before wading out to soak in the lake's waters. Dead Sea mud is so renowned for its cosmetic benefits, and reputed to aide a range of skin ailments, that it is packaged and sold around the world.

The Dead Sea lays claim to being one of the world's first health resorts. Records of people soaking in its mineral rich waters date back to the time of Herod the Great.

In ancient times, the lake was central to many of history's key events. It was where King David sought refuge from King Saul, where Abraham fought a war and (supposedly) where Ezekiel received prophecies.

Today though, the lake is not in great health. Due to damming and industrial over-usage on both sides of its Jordanian and Israeli borders, the Dead Sea is slowly shrinking. Resupply programs are being planned to grow its shoreline once more.

I plunge my hand deep into a clay pot, immersing it in the thick dark mud. Smothering it over my skin, it feels warm and sticky.

My friend with the David Attenborough voice remarks how much it reminds him of Nutella.

No one dares ask if he is basing the observation on appearance, taste, or feel on the skin as he gleefully lathers himself up.

In the distance, freshly cleaned bodies float in the water. Faces, arms and feet emerge as archipelagos of visible human form in a vast salty bathtub. A family of tourists with muddied faces standing waist-deep in the water talk and laugh.

I wade into the Dead Sea and watch as the skin on my legs begins to clear. I feel an intense burn as the waterline reaches a small cut on my knee, the salt cleaning and stinging the small wound.

I sink into the water, or at least I try to. My belly rises at once out of the water like a gluttonous iceberg, a cruel forewarning of the post-holiday diet to come. The feeling of floating is unnatural. Every time I force a limb under the water, an invisible hand pushes it back up.

The late afternoon races towards the horizon. Its rays weaken and no longer touch the whole of the valley floor. A light wind skims the lake's surface. Water ripples against my chest, pushing me gently towards the shallows. All I can see is a wide, cloudless sky...

A PALE
BLUE THAT
SEEMS TO

STRETCH
ON
FOREVER.

31

LAUTERBRUNNEN, SWITZERLAND

The sun rises early. It comes at the faded blue canvas of the tent roof with the aggression of a snarling, lycra-clad, WrestleMania character on an epic steroid binge. We are being boiled alive.

A giant witches hat from a roadwork site sits without explanation at the tent entrance. Sweat coats my forehead in a greasy, alcoholic film. There is no feeling in my right hand. Deep, dark aggressive-looking purple patches of damaged flesh mark my knees. My eyelids are crusted over and my throat burns from last night's stomach acid.

I hear Glen groan and swear in a delirium about the newly discovered perils of sleeping in an oven. Our tent looks like a working metaphor for Lindsay Lohan's acting career. It's a disaster. A train wreck of interior design with random piles of roadwork equipment, torn clothing and festering items of food and stomach contents littered throughout.

'What happened last night?' Glen asks. My mouth is dry. I struggle to get the words out.

'The Bomb Shelter... The Bomb Shelter happened last night,' is all I can say before falling out of the tent.

A group of German hikers powerwalk past my crumpled torso, crunching their rubber soles on the gravel path. They have sweatbands wrapped around their foreheads, walking poles in each hand and small camel packs full of water on their backs.

The jagged peaks of the Swiss Alps are lit orange by the blazing morning sun. I suck in greedy mouthfuls of fresh early morning mountain air. Glen stumbles out of the tent sans t-shirt but wearing a pair of wraparound sunglasses and an expression that says he will punch the world in the face if it tries to talk to him. We struggle through the centre of the camp site avoiding conversation until we have each drunk a litre of water.

'So last night hey...' Glen starts.

'Yeah, it kind of crept up on us,' I continue, 'right out of nowhere.'

Out of nowhere was about right. We had spent most of the evening pacing aimlessly around the small town of Lauterbrunnen. In depressing sobriety, we searched for anywhere that would serve us a drink.

We eventually resorted to buying a carton of warm beer from the camp site general store and dunking the cans in the glacial stream behind our tent. We had given up all hope, when a furiously drunk Kiwi stumbled out of a tent next to ours. He asked if he could steal a beer from us, slurring his words. He wondered if he'd seen us at the Bomb Shelter earlier.

'The Bomb Shelter? We didn't see that bar in town.' Glen asked.

'Nah dude, the Bomb Shelter isn't a bar. Or it is a bar, but it's not open to the public,' the Kiwi said. 'It's the cellar of an old hostel across the river. A Contiki tour group stay there most nights and they open the bar there when they do.'

'So, you're telling me there's a secret bar across the river that right now is full of drunken backpackers?' Glen spat back.

'Yeah, but it's...' The Kiwi wasn't even able to finish his sentence. We had already started running.

The Kiwi wasn't lying. The Bomb Shelter wasn't a bar. It was a stale, old cellar only a few metres wide. It had stark concrete walls, uneven flooring. There was a tiny stereo in the corner that kept stopping dead, as the extension cord was too short.

There were so many people in such a small space that it was impossible to move across the dance floor without getting an elbow in the face. The beer was warm and expensive. It smelled like someone had pissed in the corner of the room.

It was perfect.

Through a soundtrack that shifted between cheese-laden Euro disco and moments of stark silence when the power cord was pulled, Glen and I drank our way through the Bomb Shelter's limited menu. We talked to a suspicious Contiki guide who didn't remember us being in their group. We braved flying elbows on the dance floor.

We even took it in turns to unsuccessfully flirt with the local girl behind the bar. I joked to her that should the world erupt in nuclear war, at least we were safe in a bomb shelter.

'No,' she deadpanned, unfazed by the world's end.

'This isn't the actual bomb shelter. The entrance for that is around the other side of the building.'

Between serving shots of cheap vodka in small plastic cups, Unfazed by the End of the World explained, 'In Switzerland, every town must have enough bomb shelters to accommodate residents.

Also, the tunnels and bridges into and out of our country can all be blown up within eight hours. This would seal our borders against any invading force,' she said.

This was alarming news.

The Swiss have a reputation as some of the most sensible, if not boring, people in Europe. To find out that they were in fact mass-explosive-toting conspiracy theorists, preparing for the world's end with underground bunkers like a giant suicide cult, was instantly worrying.

The air in the Bomb Shelter was thick with body odour and suspicious-smelling cigarettes.

Eventually, the small bar was drunk dry of all its alcohol, so we stumbled outside. A torrent of water tumbled violently down the Staubbach Falls.

The descending water was lit silver in the moonlight and sounded like an aeroplane taking off.

Glen picked up a bright orange witches hat from the roadside.

I fell unceremoniously into a ditch.

Suddenly, a wooden window was thrown open. An old lady yelled at us to be quiet. I looked at Glen in shock. The old lady was making an entirely reasonable request. We decided on a different course of action, however. We ran away.

As we approached a bridge close to the camping grounds, we came across a man walking his dog.

The dog barked. It bared its teeth and snarled as its owner screeched at us to return the roadwork equipment. Immediately.

I turned and yelled at Glen to hurry. The last thing we needed was for the locals to confuse us with an invading force of drunken naturalists set to conquer their country under the cover of darkness.

'Hurry up,' I shouted. 'We need to cross the bridge before they blow the bloody thing up!'

FLANN
WONDI

32 PORTLAND, USA

ELETTE RLAND

The road is a picture of urban decay. The sound of a distant bassline reverberates off the rusted metal facade of an auto mechanics. The roofs of crumbling red-brick terrace houses bathe in the afternoon light.

Dan and I buy warm beer from a neighbourhood bodega. The skinny store clerk has the light smudge of a moustache on his upper lip. He could easily be 13… or 35. He scans the beer and apologises softly, barely audible over a Latin American music video.

Barely a Moustache explains that, 'The refrigerator isn't working. Sorry. But also, there's no discounts if anything that should be cold, is warm.'

I nod and swallow a complaint. I make a point of not asking if he should keep selling the tuna salad that has a thick, humid sweat forming on its clear plastic lid.

I take a sip of my room-temperature beer and it's like drinking dregs from an old ashtray left out in the rain. Dan, says that taking big mouthfuls make it easier, 'Just like ripping off a bandaid.' Dan lies. The huge gulps of beer make me gassy and I burp for two minutes straight.

There is a line about 50 metres long outside the warehouse. Inside a sweaty crowd of scantily clad college kids rub shoulders on an open-air dance floor with disco-loving divas and handlebar moustached-lumberjacks, who have clearly never lobotomised a tree in their lives.

Dan leans over, beaming, 'I couldn't think of anywhere else I'd rather be right now.'

I AGREE, I DIDN'T CHUG A GALLON OF PISS-WARM BEER FOR NOTHING.

For many years, Portland was overlooked and underappreciated. Growing up, the only thing I knew about the city was that Clyde Drexler played for the Portland Trail Blazers in NBA Jam. Like a Tinder date whose main personality fault was talking about their cryptocurrency portfolio, Portland was pleasantly unmemorable.

However, that changed when the hipsters moved in. With their painstakingly handcrafted leather goods and seasonal fruit jams, their vinyl record swap meets and home-brewed pale ales, the arrival of waves of culturally sensitive urban foragers changed Portland forever.

Gentrification and unwashed flannelette didn't just slowly appear in small pockets of the city, it consumed it.

Previously unpopulated industrial areas of Portland are now alive with warehouse conversions and community gardens. Poorly paid bicycle couriers weave through the streets, ferrying late-night food orders.

Inside the warehouse party, I drift towards the bar, desperate for hard liquor. Or mouthwash. Anything to remove the lingering sense that I just drank dirty bin water. Dan tugs on my wrist telling me we are going to a side room, where a really bad 80s cover band is about to start.

If witnessing big hair, ill-fitting leather pants and the impact of an unlimited bar tab on a middle-aged man who lives out of a 1970s station wagon has been your only experience of a tribute act in action, you've been missing out.

When done right, musical tribute bands capture the excitement of their original bands at a cut-price cost and come with the added car-crash spectacle of a group of people whose obsession has led them to the point of poorly constructed emulation.

Excited to see how bad the cover band might be, I grab my drink and push into the crowd.

Leaping onto stage in a David Bowie-ish velvet one-piece, an impossibly tall lead singer starts jumping up and down on the spot to a building drum beat. A chunky man who looks like Friar Tuck in cut-off jeans shimmies up to David Bowie. He has a keytar held to his body with an orange strap. Friar Tuck's synthesiser begins to play a familiar Van Halen introduction. I'm one of a dozen people to cheer.

The cover band are all over the stage. They make up for their lack of musical talents by running, jumping, fist pumping and working up the crowd into a singalong. The intensity of David Bowie's performance has taken its toll on his carefully manicured quiff. Greasy strands of hair fall across the singer's forehead as the band begins to murder a Tears for Fears classic.

I move outside for some air but accidentally step into a smokers' den. A nicotine-stained cloud floats above clusters of people comparing notes from their working week.

I talk with a girl with a shaved head as she carefully rolls a smoke. Shaved Head tells me she only moved to the city a few years ago and now runs a shelter rehousing abandoned cats.

I ask what it's like to live in Portland.

'It's different,' she says.

'Portland,' Shaved Head remarks, 'evolves before your eyes.'

Shaved Head explains, 'Here, what once was an abandoned car park is now a farmers' market. And what last week was a hairdresser, will soon be a speakeasy serving specialist cocktails named after bad 80s celebrity haircuts.'

I laugh and say, 'I was expecting an earnest verbal essay on how inspiring it is to live in a place surrounded by artists and makers.' Flicking her cigarette, she says, 'Don't take Portland so seriously.'

'I saw someone selling home-bound zines from a street stall yesterday,' I tell Shaved Head. 'It was bizarre. There was a DIY magazine focused on bicycle couriers coming to terms with earlobe dysmorphia after removing spacer ear-piercings.'

Shaved Head erupts in delight. 'I totally know that guy. He's so much fun. His work is hilarious!' she says.

'Whatever you do though, don't take his work literally,' she adds. 'Think of Portland as a city with a sense of humour... '

‘WHERE EVERYONE IS IN ON THE JOKE.’

NIGHTMARE AT

33

PERTH, AUSTRALIA

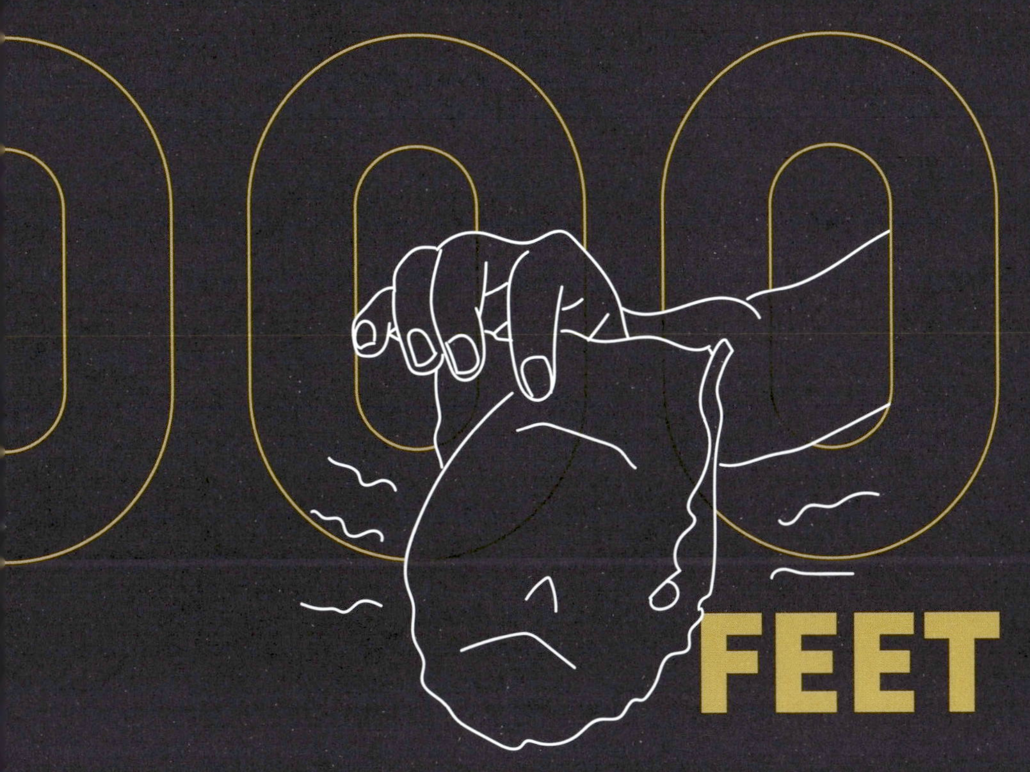
000
FEET

I once had drinks with a girl who asked about the weirdest date I had ever been on. After I told what I thought was an outrageously entertaining story, she yawned. Looked bored. Then said that the night before, over oysters and bad wine in a Carlton North restaurant, a prematurely balding man had asked her to come back to his house and shit on his chest. I never saw that girl again and had not thought much of her, until today.

It is my first time inside an airport in the age of COVID-19. The artificial lighting is harsh. Unforgiving. The bags under my eyes are clearly visible in the screen of the check-in kiosk. I struggle getting the luggage to register in the bag-drop area, but there is no one around to help. The airport is near empty, like the apocalypse had recently passed through.

A middle-aged woman waves a business-class ticket in the air and cuts the line at security. The skin on her face is pulled tight, her eyebrows arch like she is permanently surprised. I expect that her afternoons are occupied with discussions of the latest colonic hot spot over a couple of chardonnays while the Range Rover sits double-parked over the warm corpse of a golden retriever. She'd leave the dog's owner a note, but: 'Who really has the time, darling?'

It is at the departures board that I first hear it. A high-pitched whine that extends into a long howl. People turn their heads in horror. It is the sound every flyer dreads. A baby crying.

I groan and look around in frustration. I search for the screaming child, ready to condemn the parents with my eyes. Too late I remember that I am turning on the spot for no reason. The noise is coming from me. The screaming baby is strapped to my chest. It is mine.

A child makes things a bit complicated. You see, I like my travels to unfurl unplanned. I want to step out of an airport's arrival terminal without anywhere to stay and have my nose brutally assaulted by the smell of burning petrol.

I want the obnoxious urban drone of car horns, people shouting and the sounds of occasional near-death to rupture my eardrums through an open taxi window.

I drift towards pungent cities where a deep mouthful of polluted air lets you know that household garbage is not collected regularly.

I would not be surprised to one day wake up in Lima without any memory, handcuffed to an angry guinea pig in what an overzealous real estate agent would loosely describe as a 'charming fixer-upper' but a crime reporter would later call a 'crack-den house of horror.'

Bottom line, I guess you could say that the way I have travelled is not exactly kid friendly. Which is a little complicated given that I am now the co-owner of a 3-month-old boy called Alby.

My partner, Jane, readjusts her facemask and tells me to stop standing around like an idiot, 'Hurry up. We don't want to be the last ones on the flight.'

We are instructed to line up for the plane at a distance of 1.5 metres apart to practice proper social distancing, only to sit down inside the full aircraft touching shoulders with complete strangers.

There is no entertainment in the plane, outside of my personal terror of having to change Alby's nappy mid-flight and the fact he has not done a shit in two days. None of the TV systems are turned on. The airline is unable to hand out headphones, for health and safety reasons that make me question if the equipment ever even gets cleaned. Instead, I spend my time nervously watching the mood of my child and listening to a podcast I downloaded about a cult that worshipped a passing comet. They wore blue tracksuits with white sneakers the day they fulfilled their suicide pact, clearly expecting the afterlife to consist of one long Richard Simmons exercise class.

Somewhere over South Australia, at 37,000 feet in the air, I smell it. The putrid warm wafts of human excrement. Alby smiles and looks directly into my eyes, like a sadist. I hold him in the air for a closer inspection but cannot accurately tell if he has finally evacuated his bowels.

I ask Jane for a second opinion.

Jane sniffs Alby and says not to worry about changing him, he is clean. It is at that moment that I realise where the smell was coming from. It was not that Alby had unleashed World War III in his nappy, but that my own putrid breath was recycling inside my facemask. Wonderful. What I thought was the smell of baby poo was actually my breath.

The drinks cart makes its way slowly down the aisle. I ask for a glass of water, an apple juice and a coffee to try and freshen my mouth. The airline coffee shifts within its cardboard cup like the thick black sludge that washed up on the shores of Alaska following the Exxon Valdez disaster. Afterwards, my breath still smells.

‘We have movement. He’s going right now,’ Jane yells in my ear, holding our bright-red, heavily grunting boy in the air.

I grab a spare nappy, some wet wipes and a towel, before picking up Alby and moving quickly towards the one toilet I know has a change table. My heart pounds. I am living my nightmare.

I pull down the thin plastic change table inside the impossibly cramped toilet. The stink is something that could be harvested by a Third World dictator for biological weapons. Alby’s efforts overflow from his nappy, covering the change table. And me. Gagging, I taste vomit. I open the toilet door and begin to change Alby while standing in the aisle, keeping my distance, but infecting everyone around.

I apologise to a sympathetic-looking flight attendant and limp meekly back to my seat. Alby laughs and feels significantly lighter in my arms.

‘Two questions. How did he go, and did you know you have shit on your chest?’ Jane asks, pointing out a not-insignificant brown smudge across my t-shirt.

I shrug my shoulders. Instead of trying to clean my shirt, I button up the jacket I wear over it.

This is Alby’s first time flying. I cannot remember the first time I was on a plane. It would have been as a young boy going to Townsville to see family. I have not been back there since my grandfather died. Today, Townsville seems like the kind of place where an old high school classmate would establish an unsuccessful jet-ski dealership following his divorce and shares misogynistic Twitter posts on weekends.

The city of Perth bathes in a brown haze on the horizon. The pilot announces over the loudspeaker that the temperature is currently 42°C.

Jane is worried. There will be TV crews waiting at the airport. We are on the first quarantine-free flight into Western Australia in over six months and, with a new baby meeting his grandparents for the first time, we will be an irresistible lure.

Perth Airport is barely managed chaos. Jane messages her parents to ask them to wait out of sight of the cameras. Photographers circle like famished street dogs eager to pick over the carcass of human emotion. Camera lights flash with every embrace between separated family members. Reporters insert themselves into private moments.

Journalists feign sympathy, shouting, ‘How does it feel?’ But really, all they want is a 10-second newsbite for the evening lead.

Alby begins to cry. Jane pushes through the crowd I follow in her wake. We soon hear known voices. Familial hands reach out and interlock. Masks are removed and we see the faces from a years’ worth of video calls in person once again.

People push around us, but we are suddenly alone in the middle of the airport. Alby is passed to his grandmother for the first time.

'He's just beautiful. You did good, daughter,' she says, holding Alby tight. Underplaying for how long she simply wanted this moment to be.

I feel like a bystander, watching a heartfelt scene from a daytime movie. I hope no one can smell that I am still covered in shit.

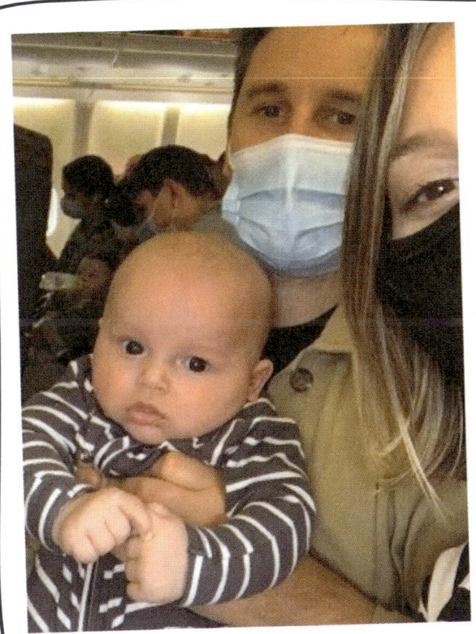

DIVE BARNAPKINS.COM
@PAUL_MANSER